This book belongs to:

_____

*a woman who desires to fulfill
God's dream for her life*

When a *Woman* Discovers Her Dream

CINDI McMENAMIN

HARVEST HOUSE PUBLISHERS

EUGENE, OREGON

Cover by Koechel Peterson & Associates, Inc., Minneapolis, Minnesota

WHEN A WOMAN DISCOVERS HER DREAM
Copyright © 2005 by Cindi McMenamin
Published by Harvest House Publishers
Eugene, Oregon 97402
www.harvesthousepublishers.com

Library of Congress Cataloging-in-Publication Data

McMenamin, Cindi, 1965-
 When a woman discovers her dream / Cindi McMenamin.
        p. cm. (pbk.)
 Includes bibliographical references.
 ISBN 0-7369-1412-9
 1. Christian women—Religious life. 2. Success—Religious aspects—Christianity. I. Title.
  BV4527.M43285 2005
  248.8'43—dc22   2004017506

Printed in the United States of America

 05 06 07 08 09 10 11 12 13 / VP-KB / 10 9 8 7 6 5 4 3 2 1

676 4753

For every woman who has dreamed of something more...
My prayer is that you'll see this book as a gift straight
from your heavenly Father's heart to yours.

Acknowledgments

With heartfelt thanks to:

- My sixth-grade schoolteacher—Mrs. Willems—my Angel of Encouragement who swooped in more than 20 years ago to save my dream when I was almost ready to give it up.

- My sister Kristi—for pursuing your dream alongside mine.

- My "sista" Chris—for continuing to see the best in me that I still can't see.

- My friend Paul—for pushing me out of my comfort zone and helping me move to a new level of trust and surrender. You always have my best at heart.

- My daughter Dana—for shining as you draw, act, dance, and sing. You prove to me that we were designed for more.

- My husband Hugh—for allowing me and encouraging me to pursue my dream, even though you hadn't yet reached yours.

And above all, I am grateful to the Lord Jesus Christ, my Dream Weaver. Without You, there would be no dream...and no reason to live it!

Contents

Once Upon a Dream

You have a dream.

We all do. Most of us have just never discovered it. Your dream may be hidden beneath layers of wounds, forgotten amidst life's circumstances or put aside due to the rush and pace of life, but nonetheless it is still there. Most of the time it waits. It waits to be discovered. To be rediscovered. Or to be hoped in again. It waits for the day you will embrace it and *really* live.

Actually, it's not so much *your* dream as it is the dream of your Maker. Like every Daddy who dreams of what his daughter will become, your Creator has a dream for you as well—a dream He had in mind when He fashioned you in the unique way that He did, when He put you in the family that He did, and when He allowed life's toll to blow your way as it did. It was all a part of His plan. And that plan—that dream He has for you—is more exciting than anything you've probably dared to imagine.

The Bible says that we are "God's masterpiece," created in Him anew so that we can do the good things He planned for us long ago.[1] We are His work of art, another translation says.

9

That means *you* are His masterpiece: His unique expression of Who He is, created before the foundation of the world to fulfill His purpose for you. To live out the dream He placed in your heart—a dream that would make you fully alive, and bring joy to your heart and your Maker's heart as well.

If God took the time to design you as the wholly unique person you are, don't think for a minute He left out what He designed you to do and be. It's written on the fabric of your heart. He's numbered our days and He's dreamed of the day you would discover—and grab hold of—the dream He has for you. Sure, He gave us choices in what we'd like to do. But let's face it, most of us settle for what life brings us. Few of us dare to dream of what God might have had in mind when He made us the unique way that we are and breathed His life into us.

From the time I was a little girl, my dream was to write books. Looking back now, I can recall the joy I experienced as I grasped the dream as a child, and the struggles I faced to hold onto that dream as a young woman. Throughout this book I'll tell my story and those of others…women just like you who have struggled, are still struggling, or have conquered the struggle to discover and live out their dream. I'm sure in one or more of these stories, you'll find *your* story, too. And I trust that in the victories, you'll be celebrating yours, as well.

You have a dream, too. But if you're like most women, your dream has remained on the shelf—untouched, long forgotten, dismissed, or simply set aside because of unforeseen circumstances, a lack of money, fear of failure, or doubt that it could possibly come true. But when you realize that dream—or rediscover it—you will come alive in new ways.

If you've ever found yourself thinking *I wish I could do more with my life,* you're not alone. If you've ever had the idea that there might be something that you're missing, there is. It's the dream you were designed to live out, but perhaps never knew about. It's the thought that nags at the back of your mind before you fall asleep at night. It's the stirring in your soul that happens every time you see someone else living out what you feel *you* are supposed to be doing. Before you hang up the dream again—feeling that it's too late, or it's too far out of reach, or it's too grand of a possibility for someone like you—it's time to take another look at what could be one of the greatest discoveries of your life. It's time to rediscover what it is you've always wanted to do, take a look at some of the reasons why, and find the roadmap to following that dream and being all you were created to be.

I have designed this book to take you step-by-step through the process of discovering your dream. How much you glean from it depends partly on how much you are willing to invest of yourself. At the end of each chapter are two sections: *Dream On* and *Press On. Dream On* is meant to provoke your thoughts and insights and help you discern your dream, as well as help you apply the principles discussed in the chapter. I encourage you to work through each question and exercise, as they are crucial to your progress from chapter to chapter. *Press On* is intended to encourage you and get you ready for what's to come.

So...are you ready? It's *not* too late to discover your dream, my friend. In fact, there's no better time than now. So, join me on this adventure of discovering, embracing, and living out your dream. And as you do, you'll see, firsthand, what incredible things can happen when a woman discovers her dream.

Part I

Discovering the Dream

*"Don't live carelessly, unthinkingly.
Make sure you understand
what the Master wants."*

—EPHESIANS 5:17 (MSG)

1
Daring to Dream Again

⟶

There are two kinds of people when it comes to discovering one's dream. Those who dare to dream. And those who've given up. Which story is yours?

"Candy" balks at the idea of discovering her dream. "Why does someone have to have a dream to pursue, anyway?" she asks, almost irritated. "Why can't people just learn to be content? I'm someone's wife and someone's mother. Isn't that enough? Why do I have to search for something *more?*" Candy's tone is almost bitter. Is it true that having a dream is a sign of discontent? Or has something deep in Candy's heart refused to let her dream anymore?

To answer Candy's question, there's nothing wrong with being content with your life. Being a wife and a mother *is* wonderful. But what was Candy *uniquely* designed to do that *only* she can do? How was she created for "good works" that God planned for her long ago? When Candy asked her questions, my response was to ask a few more: "But what about when your kids are grown? What will you do then? What if, when your husband hits midlife, he wants to pursue different goals? Then what? Our purpose in life must consist of more than our roles and relationships."

"Angie" agrees with Candy. But rather than being bitter, she is nonchalant. "I never really thought about having a dream," she said. "Since I got pregnant in high school and then got married, I just lived life the way it came. I never went to college and pursued a real career, but I'm happy with how my life turned out, anyway. I've never had this desire to have to make something of my life or accomplish some great thing. I figure you just do the best you can and if you're happy, then you did okay."

Again, there's no rule that someone must *strive for more.* But then, is our own happiness and contentment the ultimate goal? What about the contentment and pleasure of the One who made us in secret? Psalm 139:15-16 says, "My frame was not hidden from you when I was made in the secret place. When I was woven together in the depths of the earth, your eyes saw my unformed body. All the days ordained for me were written in your book before one of them came to be."

If God took such great care and detail to "weave" us together in our mothers' wombs and ordain all of our days before there were any, wouldn't He have also woven into our hearts a special purpose for us as well? And wouldn't that plan and purpose for us be as unique to us as our fingerprints? A God whom we're told counts the number of hairs on our heads (Matthew 10:30), and records our days in a book (Psalm 139:16), and saves our tears in a bottle (Psalm 56:8 NASB) surely would not just set us on this earth at random, not caring this way or that about what we do with our lives.

Perhaps for Candy or Angie, the big dream hasn't occupied much of their thoughts. But it's been on their Maker's heart...since the day they were born.

Maybe your story is that you know you have a dream. You just feel guilty sometimes for not pursuing it, or frustrated at not being able to reach it. Or perhaps you're saddened each time you see someone else living out what you feel you're supposed to do. If so, you're not alone. You're one of the countless women for which this book was written. And prayerfully, you're one of the women who will be encouraged through this book by finding what it is you are supposed to be doing.

Now, when I talk of pursuing a dream, I'm not suggesting we ignore our God-given responsibilities at home in order to pursue something that seems more exciting or fulfilling. We need to continue taking care of priorities at home, and realize that if God has given us a husband and family to care for, we are already living our part of His dream for us right now. What I *am* suggesting, however, is that He has something unique in mind for us that goes beyond what we may have considered before.

Encouragement Early On

I mentioned earlier that every Daddy has dreams for his little girl. From the time I learned to walk, my Dad was telling me I could accomplish anything. He constantly told me how smart I was (which came in handy by the time the "blonde" jokes started rolling around in my adulthood), and he often bragged about his "Ceenee" and that she would "go places." I guess that instilled in me a confidence to dream big, set goals, make plans. To this day, every New Year's Day, I sit with pen in hand and write out what I hope to accomplish in the next year—physically, financially, vocationally, educationally, and spiritually.

It wasn't so with my older sister, however. Although she was as smart as I was (probably even more so), and twice as able in many areas, she didn't receive the encouragement I did. Kristi, at the age of 5, could pick up any instrument and play it by ear. She had an exceptional ear for music, an exceptional vocal range, could sing any part, and hit any note in the spectrum. I, on the other hand, couldn't carry a tune for most of my childhood. But because Kristi didn't excel academically (meaning she didn't get straight As like I did) she was in some ways, although not intentionally, dismissed in terms of academic expectations. No one encouraged Kristi to go to college or strive for more. For years, Kristi struggled with trying to figure out what others wanted her to do, what it was *she* wanted to do, or what it was that might bring in some extra income. And then the day came—at 40 years old—when she discovered her dream and dared to pursue it...not for her parents or her husband or her children or her friends. Not even for her, but for her Lord. After all, it was *His* dream for her. (I tell her inspiring story in chapter 7.)

It's Not About Us

When we get past our own hesitation to dream, our baggage at what may have hindered the pursuit of our dream, and our fear or reluctance to think outside the box, we can begin to listen for the dream that God placed on our hearts when He wove us together. After all, He continues to whisper the dream to us so that we'll

> *We cannot separate the dream from the One who has whispered that dream on our heart.*

respond...and bring Him joy as we live out the dream He intended for us to live. The bottom line is that it's not about us. It's about the One who made us and what *He* had in mind.

As we talk about discovering a dream, it's important for us to realize that finding this dream is not primarily so we can be happy. And it's not so we can feel significant or have the satisfaction of knowing we're living out our purpose. Those are all *benefits* of living out our dream, but they are not *the motivation* and reason behind discovering it. Our motivation is to fulfill the call that God has placed on our lives and live out for Him what He intended, for His glory.

As Os Guinness writes in his book *The Call,* "First and foremost we are called to Someone (God), not to something (such as motherhood, politics, or teaching) or to somewhere (such as the inner city of Outer Mongolia)."[1] That is our primary calling—to love and obey God (Matthew 22:37). Our secondary or specific calling is *how* we carry out our expression of love for God—through thinking, speaking, living, and acting entirely for Him. We cannot separate the dream from the One who has whispered that dream on our heart. If there is no Dream Giver, there is no dream. If there is no Caller, there is no calling. If there is no Creator, there is no reason to continue.

If you're still not too sure about a Creator who's designed a dream for you, that's okay. Stay with me anyway. I'm confident that as you continue this search, you will find more than a dream. You will find the Dream Giver, who stands offering you not only the dream, but life eternal...and life to the full.[2] And hopefully, on this journey, you will experience what Guinness describes: "We start out searching, but we end up being discovered. We think we are looking for something; we realize we are found by Someone."[3]

Where Do You Stand?

So which story is yours when it comes to discovering the dream that God has whispered on your heart? Are you the skeptic? (Probably not. After all, you've picked up this book, haven't you?) Are you the "innocence is bliss" type who doesn't know your dream and doesn't really care, you're just happy anyway? Are you the one who is beginning to struggle because you *know* there is something more but you just don't know where to start? Or are you someone who knows what your dream is, but you are still trying to grasp hold of it?

Regardless of where you are on the journey, this is the place to start.

Looking Back on the Dream

One of the best ways to discover what it is you were called to do is to think back to the time when you were a little girl. What is it you wanted to be when you grew up? A princess? A ballerina? An actress? A nurse? A model? A mommy?

Whenever I speak to women's groups on this topic, and ask them to think back to what they wanted to be as little girls, many women in the audience begin to cry. Something tugs at their hearts as I ask them to recall what it is they've always wanted to do. Perhaps as we recall our childhood, we remember that a dream was there, and we so long to get it back. Or, maybe as we think back to days long ago, we encounter wounds that struck our hearts, shattered our innocence, and kept us from pursuing what it was we wanted to do. I'm going to talk about that in the next chapter. But for now, try to think of what you told others you wanted to be when you grew up.

Maybe you're embarrassed to say. I remember telling people I wanted to be a librarian. My husband laughs when I say this. He can't imagine me being in a profession in which I have to be quiet most of the day. But I can see today that my love for the library, and wanting to be there, was because of my love for books. I wanted to read them, be around them, take care of them, write them.

I also wanted to be a schoolteacher. In fact, I had it figured out that I would be a schoolteacher during the school year and a librarian during the summers, when school was out. Then during my junior high and high school years, I even toyed with the idea of being a cosmetologist.

Looking back now I can see that I not only had a love for books (the writer in me), but also a love to teach (which is the speaker and Bible teacher in me). And could it be that I wanted to be a cosmetologist because I had a desire to help women become beautiful, or at least all they could be? I imagine God looking at all those desires I had while growing up and smiling as He knew back then that I would someday live out His dream for me...to be a writer who speaks and teaches, and helps other women see how beautiful they are in the eyes of God. While I was growing up, I had no idea that those desires I had for my future were rooted in a desire God had already put in my heart to be something I had yet to discover. I just figured I had three different ideas of what I would like to do with my life. Perhaps, as a child, I was simply unknowingly expressing the dream that was on my heart.

What did *you* want to be when you were a little girl? Think about that for a few moments, and record your answer here:

_____

_____

_____

Now ask a parent, sibling, or a close friend with whom you grew up if they remember what it was you often talked about becoming back when you were a child. Write their answer here:

Ask that person, also, what it was you often spent your time doing (and playing) as a child. Record their answer here:

Looking at how you spent your time as a child can be eye-opening when it comes to discerning the dream that God placed on your heart. That's because when we were children, we tended to live from our hearts. We most likely did things because we *wanted* to, not because we felt we had to, which is how we tend to live our lives as adults. What was going on as your heart (and the Maker of your heart) was trying to communicate to you your dream? Think about it...and begin the exciting process of discovering your dream.

You're not the *only one* who's been waiting for this day to arrive....

~ *Dream On* ~

what would you love to be
r or calling?_____

_____

_____

when you were a child and
e doing as you grew up is
ure, residues of that dream
ce it may have been awhile
hat it is you were designed
g, try this.

ircle the words that really

build	call
complete	compose
delight	demonstrate
distribute	dream
engage	enhance
explore	express
foster	further
grant	heal
illuminate	implement
ntegrate	involve	know

labor	launch	lead	live	love
make	manifest	measure	mediate	model
motivate	negotiate	nurture	open	organize
participate	persuade	praise	prepare	promote
pursue	realize	reclaim	reflect	release
renew	resonate	restore	satisfy	save
serve	share	speak	support	surrender
sustain	team	touch	translate	travel
understand	use	validate	value	venture
volunteer	work	worship	write	yield

Now narrow your choices down to the three verbs that are the most meaningful and purposeful to you, and write them in the blanks below:

_____, _____ and _____

Step 2

Next, think about what you stand for, what your cause is, or what you'd be willing to devote your life to or even die for. Would it be family values, or truth, or God's Word, or justice? Think about your passion (which literally means what you'd be willing to suffer for), and then insert that word or phrase here:

_____

Step 3

Our dream is never about just us. Who is it you are being called to help or serve? Who is it that stands to benefit from you living out your dream? Is it children? Women? The elderly? Think about it and write that one group, entity, or cause you would most like to help or impact in a positive way:

_____

Step 4

Now put the puzzle pieces together.
My dream is to:

_____, _____ and _____
(your three verbs)

_____
(your cause or value)

to, for, or with

_____
(the group or cause that most moves you)

Some people refer to this kind of statement as their mission statement for life. For now, we'll call it your basic dream concept. We'll build from here to discover the specifics of just *how* you will accomplish the statement above—if it truly represents, or is beginning to sound like, your dream.

When I completed this exercise six years ago, I came up with the following:

To encourage, inspire, and motivate Christlikeness in women. I later added the "how" element with the phrase "through writing, speaking, and teaching." That became the grid through which I passed everything through. If I was asked to partake in an extra-curricular activity, I asked myself if it somehow fit into my purpose statement. If it did, I pursued it. If not, I suggested someone else. That statement has also reinforced to me what it is I need to focus on. And your statement will be a catalyst for you, too, in taking one more step down the road toward discovering your dream.

Well, are you feeling a bit closer to discovering the dream God whispered on your heart? If not, stick with me. We're just beginning on this journey. There's much more to the exciting adventure ahead.

⌒ *Press On* ⌒

Psalm 37:5 says, "Commit your way to the LORD; trust in him and he will do this." Another translation of that verse reads, "Open up before God, keep nothing back; he'll do whatever needs to be done: He'll validate your life in the clear light of day and stamp you with approval at high noon" (MSG).

Isn't it exciting to finally have a few words that may help describe the dream that's been whispered on your heart? Now that you've come up with your basic dream concept, let's look next at the forces that may be working to keep you from wholeheartedly embracing your dream.

"Set me free from my prison, that I may praise your name. Then the righteous will gather about me because of your goodness to me."

—Psalm 142:7

2

Dismissing the Dream Destroyer

$\mathcal{I}$f you've always wanted to paint, why aren't you?

If you once dreamed of becoming a dancer, what stopped the pursuit?

We never really outgrow our dreams. Most of the time, they're snatched away from us by someone who blurted out cruel words, or looks, or laughs, and obviously didn't know better.

What was once said to *you* that might have destroyed your dream as it was just beginning to take shape?

When my daughter, Dana, was only four, an older child in her Sunday school class blurted out carelessly (as many children do): "You don't color good." For several months after that, every time Dana picked up a crayon she apologized before starting: "I can't color very good, Dad, but I'll try." My husband was the one who first noticed her self-condemnation.

"Dana, why do you think you don't color well?" he asked tenderly.

"I don't know, I just don't," she answered, self-consciously.

"Dana, who *told* you that you can't color very well?" her Daddy persisted.

The truth came out in tears.

"Sabrina said I always go outside the lines and I'm real messy. She got mad at me for messing up her book."

There it was. Five-year-old Sabrina, who wasn't capable of many other things at that age, was perfectly able to destroy a dream in little Dana's heart to someday be an artist.

After that, we poured into Dana loads of encouragement every time we saw her pick up a pencil, pen, paintbrush, or crayon. We bought her buckets of sidewalk chalk and encouraged her to decorate the neighborhood. And after more than a year of constant praise, the heaps of positive encouragement replaced that single negative message. Today Dana draws, paints, colors, and designs things. She can take a pipe cleaner and shape it into a movie character. She can design a microphone with aluminum foil and a paper clip. She can fold a single sheet of lined paper into a three-dimensional box with fancy, curved edges. And she confidently told her sixth grade class recently that she plans to be an artist when she grows up, just like her Uncle Steven. Fortunately for Dana, her dream was rescued while she was young enough to keep dreaming.

Who Are the Dream Destroyers?

Dream destroyers are everywhere. They can wear the disguise of our parents, teachers, spouse, best friend, a stranger, or even a five-year-old girl named Sabrina. Chances are you had a dream destroyer in your life as well. Maybe you didn't necessarily want to be an artist, but simply hearing someone say you couldn't color made you shy away from creating *anything*. I know a beautiful woman who wanted to be a ballerina but she was once told, "You could *never* dance with that kind of body!"

Probably one of the most common fears among adults today is that of being in front of a crowd. I have several friends who get physically sick at the mere thought of standing up and addressing a group of people. I often wonder if nearly everyone who fears this has had some sort of past criticism, embarrassing moment, or perceived failure that now makes them want to avoid any situation that opens the potential for embarrassment in front of others.

∽◌

Sometimes if you think back to the deepest wound in your past, there you find your dream. Why? Because the chief Dream Destroyer (Satan, whom I'll also refer to as the enemy) would like nothing more than to deter you from your dream, as a way of getting back at your Maker. Ever since Satan was thrown out of heaven for wanting to be equal with God (Isaiah 14:12-15), he has wanted to get even with the Almighty. But Satan, a created being, is no match for God. So if he can't get back at God directly, he'll try to get back at God indirectly—by going through those whom God loves. Yet God often puts a hedge of protection around His own. So if Satan can't get to us directly, he'll go after our dream. What better way to crush the Maker's heart than to crush the potential of what God's little girl will become? I believe in many cases, the enemy makes attempts to kill our dream while we're young and vulnerable and unable to see what he's really doing. That's why if you want to discover your dream, it's possible you'll find it by going back to your deepest wound.

When I shared that at a conference recently, a woman I'll call "Barbara" came up to me afterward and, in tears, told me her story. It consisted of her greatest wound…and as she relived it, she found, underneath the layers of the wound, her dream.

Barbara's Story

"As far back as I can remember, I loved playing the piano," Barbara told me. "I recall sitting at the piano for hours, making up songs and singing them to Jesus and to my sisters and brothers. Then one day I came home from school to find our family piano being loaded onto a truck. My parents said they had sold it because it was "too big" for the house. I remember crying and screaming 'No!' as the truck pulled out of the driveway, carrying the piano away. 'Please don't take away my piano,' I cried, screaming at the top of my lungs. And as I stood in the driveway crying my lungs out, long after the truck left, no one cared."

Barbara had long since forgotten that part of her childhood. Until that weekend at the women's retreat. She had been watching the worship director and thinking to herself, *I would love to lead women in worship at a retreat like this.* Then when she heard me talk about our wounds and ask the women to think back to their most painful childhood memory, she remembered the piano—*and her dream.*

"I remember what my dream was," she told me, her eyes sparkling. "I loved to play the piano and worship. And that's why I was so captivated this weekend with the worship leader and how she played and worshiped God. That's why I was feeling that I *needed* to be doing that someday."

I challenged Barbara with the next step: "What are you going to do now?" I asked.

"As soon as I get home, I'm going to find a piano teacher. I'm over 40, but I'm going to start taking piano lessons," she said, smiling. At the midpoint of her life, Barbara had rediscovered her dream. And I can't help but think her Maker was rejoicing that day, too.

Debbie's Dream

"Debbie" loved to sing. But when she sang her first solo in her church's choir, she received an insensitive comment afterward from another woman in the choir. "It's not all about *you,*" the woman said cattily. Debbie was so devastated that someone got the impression that she was singing to show off herself that she quit singing. Ten years went by and Debbie held the pain and shame within her every time she heard someone sing a solo or talk to her about singing again. "Because that one woman had implied that I did it for myself, and for my glory, I felt so ashamed and thought, *If that's what people think when I sing, then I shouldn't do it at all.* And I didn't for ten years. Now I realize that the Dream Destroyer didn't want me singing because that's what God wanted me doing."

"What are you going to do now?" I asked Debbie.

Her answer came as quickly as Barbara's: "I'd like to start taking voice lessons," she said. As God would have it, my sister, a trained vocal coach who had just started teaching private voice lessons, was there at the conference as well. "I'd like you to meet someone," I told Debbie and introduced her to my sister. Debbie started voice lessons the next week and took one giant step toward reclaiming the dream God had placed on her heart.

What has deterred *you* from your dream? An insensitive or hurtful comment? Parents who failed to encourage you? Repeated circumstances that convinced you that you could never reach your goal or dream?

Retracing My Own Wound

I was a senior in high school when the Dream Destroyer came after my dream. But what happened was so very subtle that I didn't realize what had taken place until years later.

I was the editor of my high school newspaper, had won numerous writing contests, and was well on my way to being a journalist. I loved to write. And evidently God had been confirming that all my life. I felt privileged to know, at the tender age of 17, what I was going to do with the rest of my life. I had already applied to colleges to major in journalism. Then the arrow was launched, most unexpectedly.

I was taking an honors English class my first semester of my senior year. I knew the teacher was an outspoken atheist and was told that anyone who believed in God might have trouble in his class. But I prayed about taking the class and believed it would help strengthen me academically as well as spiritually.

After writing and turning in my first paper for the class, the teacher pulled me aside for a talk. Compassionately, he told me his comments might be hard for me to hear, but he wanted to do all he could to help me.

"Cindi, you *can't* write," he said, with a look of concern in his eyes. "You make basic mistakes in sentence construction and you stumble through themes and supporting arguments. What are you doing majoring in journalism?"

Shocked, I look at him in disbelief. "What are you talking about?" I asked. "I've gotten straight *A*s in writing and English for as far back as I can remember. My journalism adviser said I was the top writer in the class; that's why he made me editor of the school paper. I've won awards for essays and speeches I've written. If I can't write, why am I just now hearing about it?"

My teacher shook his head and said I was a classic example of the low standards in the state's public educational system. "You've gotten As because your writing was maybe a little better than others, but it's still not exceptional. Not enough for you to write as a career. I strongly suggest you rethink your direction." He put his arm around me and looked as if he had compassion for me. "I know this is hard for you to hear. But I really do want to keep you from making one of the biggest mistakes of your life."

Shattered, I left school that day in a daze. And I did the only thing I could think of doing: I went to visit my sixth grade teacher, who was still teaching at the junior high school across town—the same woman who encouraged me to shoot for my goals, aim high, be more than what others tell me I can be. In the six months that she taught me (coming in at the middle of my sixth grade year), she poured more encouragement into me than I had received the first 12 years of my life. I felt she loved me like her own daughter. I knew she'd level with me. So I went to see Mrs. Willems.

I waited for her outside her classroom that afternoon, and when she saw me by the door, she lit up momentarily. Then upon noticing my downcast countenance, she immediately asked, "What's wrong?" In tears, I recounted everything I was told by my honors English teacher that day. "Why didn't you tell me?" I asked. "Am I really as bad as he says?" Mrs. Willems didn't say a word. Instead, she turned around and walked straight to her file cabinet and took out a folder she'd saved for the past six years.

.ed this day might come, so I've been saving this," she
.tly. She pulled out my state aptitude test scores as a sixth
"These show your academic aptitude, compared to students
across the nation," she said. "As a sixth grader, your English com-
prehension and vocabulary skills were at the eleventh-grade level.
And your writing scores, even as a 12-year-old, were off the charts.

"You *can* write, Cindi," she told me very firmly. "Someone just
doesn't want you to."

∽

After a discussion with my parents that evening and much
prayer, I transferred out of that honors English class at the end of
the semester and humbly took my first-ever C- on my quarterly
report card. It was true someone didn't want me to write. But
Someone Else still did.

Looking back at that situation, it's easy for me to believe that
the enemy was attempting to take me out early. I'm so thankful for
my angel of a teacher, Mrs. Willems, who came to the rescue when
the dream on my heart was about to be discouraged from coming
to fruition.

I wonder what would've happened if I hadn't gone to
Mrs. Willems that day? Would I have let one person determine
my destiny? Yet, so many of us do just that.

Recognizing Dream Destroyers

Can you recall a deep hurt that made you, knowingly or
unknowingly, give up your dream?

Maybe it wasn't any one person who destroyed your dream.
Maybe it was discouragement that came in another form, or several

forms. There are three primary dream destroyers. If you know what they are, you might be able to put your finger on which one tried or is still trying to steal your dream away.

> *If it's God's dream for us, nothing can stop it from being realized.*

Fears and Doubts—These usually come in the form of what's called "negative self talk" or discouraging thoughts. *I'll never be able to do that. It'll take too much time (money, effort). Why should I think something like that could happen to me? I'll surely fail and embarrass myself and those around me. What if I can't do it?* It's natural for us to beat ourselves up or to lack confidence that we can achieve something. But if it's God's dream for us, nothing can stop it from being realized. That should take the pressure off of us. Instead of negatively thinking *I can't do this*, start thinking in terms of *He surely can do this in me.*

Discouragement from Others—When others discourage us, I believe it's mostly unintentional. Many times other people around us feel the need to give us a "dose of reality" to keep us from getting our hopes up and then being disappointed. I remember many people telling me, "Everyone wants to get published; don't get your hopes up." I truly believe they were trying to be helpful. But I needed cheerleaders, not doomsayers. Fortunately I learned to not take their words to heart. I filtered out their comments with the hopeful thought, *But in my case, it's different. He's the One who will make it happen.* We must learn to weigh the many times God affirms our dream against the unsupportive comments we receive so we can go back to what we know we're supposed to do.

Attempts from the Enemy—Satan will sometimes work through our circumstances in an attempt to dissuade us from our dream and try to make us give it up. Take Bonnie, for example. Hers is a story in which the enemy was actively trying to snuff out her dream for years.

Overcoming the Obstacles

Fifty-three-year-old Bonnie always knew what she wanted to do.

"As a little girl, I always wanted to be in dance and perform," Bonnie recalls.

However, there were ten children in her family and her parents couldn't afford to give her dance lessons. Fortunately, Bonnie had a friend in junior high school who took classes in every form of dance, and her friend ended up teaching Bonnie to dance as well. The two performed at Christmas banquets for underprivileged children, the high school football banquet, and other local functions.

When she got into high school, Bonnie tried out for the drill team and won a spot on the team. But her family ended up moving away just after the school year started and she was never able to perform with the team. Looking back now, she saw that as the first arrow that was launched to kill her dream.

When she was 30, Bonnie married and was living in Cincinnati and auditioned for the Cincinnati Bengals cheerleading squad and made the team. But her husband got a job transfer and they moved before she got a chance to perform with the team. Needless to say, the second arrow had been launched.

Several years later, she moved to Dallas. She auditioned for the Dallas Cowboys' cheerleading squad, but she didn't make the squad and figured her dance days were over. She ended up teaching aerobics for six years for exercise guru Richard Simmons. As she taught overweight women, she discovered her passion—helping women overcome their doubts and low self-esteem issues and gain a sense of confidence through weight loss and better nutrition. Just as she began thinking about pouring her heart into her passion, she discovered that she had nerve damage in her feet, which had been caused by working a couple jobs where she was on her feet constantly. She eventually found herself in constant pain. The third arrow had been launched.

"The enemy doesn't want to see me fulfill my dream and he doesn't want to see those women free either," Bonnie told me recently. Fortunately, the physical obstacle of her foot pain will not stand in the way of her dream.

"Every time I try to push the dream away and say 'I can't,' God always stirs up the dream again—through a sermon at church, something I hear on the radio, or even a book that someone sends me. God keeps reminding me of the dream."

And during this time in which she is dealing with foot pain, Bonnie optimistically says, "This is my time of resting in Him.

"I'm waiting on God to heal my feet or to expand the dream to what He wants it to look like. God may want me to speak to women's groups on encouraging them in their weight loss," she said, "rather than actually leading them on the exercise floor.

"I think the dream God has given me has been expanded. The desire to dance is still there. I'm still waiting to see how that's a part of it. But He may want the dream to look different than I have always seen it."

Today Bonnie understands that her dream is actually to "encourage worthiness" among women. As a host of a Christian radio station in Dallas, she constantly interviews authors and celebrities who are encouraging others, and she has radio air time in which she is able to offer sound words of encouragement, as well.

"What I'm doing now is a part of the dream, but a different avenue," Bonnie says. She now realizes that encouraging women through exercise and nutrition was *her* vision of how the dream could be expressed or carried out. But her work through the radio station may be God's preference in how her dream is to be expressed.

As Bonnie recounted her story, it was clear there was a Dream Destroyer at work. Some people call it circumstances or tough breaks. But after having heard countless stories of the dream and how it almost slipped away, I've become more and more convinced that there is a Dream Destroyer at work. And he means business.

Although the Dream Destroyer was actively trying to keep Bonnie from fulfilling her dream, by discouraging her through the constant missed opportunities and the constant pain in her feet, he wasn't able to kill the passion in her heart to see women become whole. I love how the Dream Weaver kept reminding Bonnie of her dream and wooing her back to a place of hope and waiting on Him.

∽∾

Another lesson we can learn from Bonnie is that when we look at our dream, we have to remember that God's plan might look different from ours.

For example, I wanted to write…and I thought my first book would be called *Pathway to a Prince* about how to find the perfect husband. Yet, God's way was for me to be disillusioned with the happily-ever-after and write a book for women about how to be fulfilled in the way God Himself is our husband. My ministry is still writing, but my writing often addresses how to cope with what goes wrong in a woman's life...rather than a "how to" in doing everything right!

Don't Lose Heart!

Though the Dream Destroyer may try to seemingly rob us of opportunities to fulfill our dream, with God's help, we can find a way. The enemy could wound Bonnie's feet, but he couldn't prevent her from opportunities that allowed her to help women become whole. So be encouraged, my friend. Your dream is still out there...waiting for you to grab hold of it. Not even the Destroyer can pry it completely from your heart. And God will bring about the fulfillment in the form He knows is best. Your dream may come to fruition in a way you don't expect.

Perhaps you've remembered some arrows that were launched into your heart, attempting to take your dream away. Perhaps you've realized that some people have unintentionally deterred you from your dream. Don't lose heart. Recognizing the Dream Destroyer and seeing his attempts for what they are is another step in the right direction toward discovering and pursuing your dream.

Are you feeling a sense of relief at knowing you do indeed still have a dream that is alive and well? Take heart in knowing that your Dream Maker rejoices with you....

~ *Dream On* ~

1. What is the deepest wound you can remember as a child?

    (If this is too painful to revisit, think of it in terms of an exercise in setting your heart free. If you were victimized in some way, that was an attempt by the enemy to shut you down in some way or other. This is an effort to get you back on track with where your Maker designed you to be.)

2. What types of activities, if any, has that wound prevented you from doing?

3. What do you feel you're *not* good at, and why?

4. What did you once love to do but haven't done in awhile? Why have you not done it?

5. What would it take to start it up again?

In chapter 1, you came up with your basic dream concept. If through this chapter you have rediscovered what it is you once loved to do or have always wanted to do, it may be time to add it to your statement. If you know it already, skip down to the statement, recopy the words from page 25, and add on the last line what it is you've always wanted to do. If you still aren't sure, look through these words to determine just *how* you might live out your cause. Circle one, two, or three words that represent what you'd most like to *do*.

helping	serving	cooking	sewing	decorating ,
coaching	playing	leading	assisting	encouraging
cleaning	organizing	acting	dancing	drawing
performing	singing	painting	giving	writing
speaking	teaching			

Now narrow your choice to one word, if you can. Write that one word here that most excites you:

_____

Now recopy your basic dream concept from page 25, and add in the last line (from the exercise above).

Now put the puzzle pieces together.
My dream is to:

_____, _____, and _____
(your three verbs)

_____
(your cause or value)
to, for, or with

_____

(the group or cause that most moves you)

by or through

_____

(the one word that most excites you)

~ *Press On* ~

Rejoice, my friend, because there is hope. Much more powerful than any Dream Destroyer is the redeeming Life Giver who promises in His Word to work all things (even the bad things) together for good in our life when we love Him and are called to His purposes (Romans 8:28). In chapter 3, we'll look at how God can use those things in our life that we thought were absolutely unusable...and how they make up the beauty—that's right, the beauty—of who we are today.

"God made my life complete when I placed all the pieces before him. When I got my act together, he gave me a fresh start.... God rewrote the text of my life when I opened the book of my heart to his eyes."

—Psalm 18:20-24 (MSG)

3

Discovering Your True Potential

What is *your* dream?" Kelly asked, beaming as she looked into the camera, addressing the television audience. She was hosting a Christian television show that featured one woman's dream and how it turned into a ministry.

After the show, I asked Kelly to tell me about *her* dream. And I was surprised at what I learned. Not only was this African-American beauty actually living out her dream of being a witness for God in the entertainment industry, but at one time she believed that because of her mistakes and the pit she was living in, her life would never amount to anything.

"When I was a kid, I used to write plays and skits and make everyone in the family put them on," Kelly recalls. "I knew I wanted to be involved in the creative arts. I'd dance around the house and make my father dance with me. That was what I always wanted to do."

Kelly's eyes shone as she recalled those days when, as a little girl, she knew clearly what she wanted to be. But her smile faded as she started to recount the obstacles she hit and the ugliness that took over her life as she got older.

When she was 15 years old and living in Long Island, Kelly got involved in the entertainment industry, modeling and appearing in commercials. She was asked to audition for the movie *Fame* and became one of the three finalists for the part that ultimately went to Janet Jackson. After appearing in 80 national and regional commercials, guest-starring on "Sesame Street" and soap operas like "All My Children" and "Another World," and starring in some ABC specials and independent films, Kelly moved to Southern California to further her acting career. But the film industry in California became a stumbling block to her.

"The atmosphere of sex and drugs was so bad," she said. "By the time I was 18, I was very promiscuous and ended up getting pregnant. I had an abortion and got pregnant again three months later. I didn't want to have another abortion, because it was the worst experience I'd ever had, so I kept the baby."

Kelly's parents were devastated. She couldn't go to college anymore. She couldn't pursue her acting and modeling career. She ended up living with her parents, was on welfare, and struggled to make ends meet. She described her life as being "in the pit" and said she even prostituted her body for money during that time.

By the time her child was three years old, Kelly was drowning in despair. And she was wrought with fear. She had been dabbling with New Age religion, looking for answers and purpose, but still feeling hopeless. It was at that point that she surrendered her life to God and asked Him to take away her fear and redeem her life. She threw away her New Age trinkets and cried out to God in desperation, pleading, "God, can you *please* put it all back together?"

To her surprise, He did. She enrolled in a community college and through her new faith in God and dependence on Him, she put her whole heart into her schoolwork. As a single mother, Kelly ended up being the first African-American valedictorian of the school. She graduated from Nassau Community College with $15,000 in scholarships and then received a full scholarship to Hofstra University in New York, the school she originally wanted to attend before she got pregnant with her first child.

After graduating from the community college, Kelly married and started at Hofstra, but got pregnant with her second and third child while there. Having the babies caused her to put on hold her dream of continuing her education and pursuing a major in music. But by the time her third child was a year old, the school reinstated her scholarship and she continued to study music. She picked up her violin, which she hadn't played for nearly 10 years, and sensed God's blessing as she began to excel again. Kelly's life started looking like it was coming back together. She received all the top music honors and scholarships and made a CD. But all the while, her dream was still to work in the entertainment industry. Because of the notoriety she received as a musician, Kelly got the attention of an acting agency once again.

Kelly then signed with a top agency in New York. "At my first photo shoot, I felt awful. I thought, *Here I am, a Christian, doing this photo shoot wearing hardly anything at all.*" After the shoot she felt discouraged, and while praying one day, she sensed the Lord telling her to cancel her contract with the agency.

Kelly cancelled the contract and in doing so, handed her dream back to God, figuring that He didn't want her near the entertainment industry again. Because of what she did, she was told, "You'll never work again." But three weeks later, Kelly sensed

God telling her to send her resumé and picture to three Christian television stations, in hopes of becoming a TV anchorwoman.

"I hadn't yet thought of broadcasting," she said. "Out of obedience, I sent out my resumé, not thinking anything would happen."

Two of the stations contacted her and told her they had nothing available. But the third station, in Indiana, called and said, "We're interested, but you have no credentials." Kelly responded by saying, "I'm just doing what the Lord told me to do." She was told to come be a guest on the show.

"Little God-things happened," Kelly said. As it turns out, she was hired to host one of the shows. Her producer later told her, "We were just about to hire someone else when your package came."

"I'm now living out my dream," "Kelly said, smiling from ear to ear. "And I can't even take credit for it. I didn't know anything about broadcasting or producing." But Kelly did know a God who could take the pieces of her life and put them back together again as she surrendered her hopes and dreams to Him.

It's Never Too Late

Kelly believed at one time that her mistakes marred her chances of experiencing something more. But that was before Kelly had met her Redeemer, the Dream Weaver...who is also a Master Artist, One who specializes in taking corrupted canvases and repainting them into magnificent masterpieces.

Have you ever thought of yourself as a masterpiece? In Ephesians 2:10, we are told that we are God's masterpiece, created anew in Christ Jesus "so that we can do the good things he planned for us long ago" (NLT). The word *masterpiece* (which in some versions of the Bible is translated *workmanship*) comes from the Greek word *poiema,* from which we get our English word "poem." Another way of reading that verse is this: We are God's poem...created anew in Christ Jesus (when we surrender our lives to Him) for great works that He planned for us long ago.

Think about the beauty and uniqueness of a poem or sonnet. A poem is one's unique expression of who they are and what they want to say. And God says that each of us who have been born anew through faith in Christ is *His* poem—*His* unique expression of who He is and what He wants to say. Wow!

You Are God's Poem

You are God's work of art, too. No matter what has happened in your life, no matter what mistakes you might have made, no matter where you've been or how you might have messed up, God can redeem your life, restore it, and transform it into a breathtakingly beautiful masterpiece.

When I talk to women about being God's masterpiece, I know there are some who think, *I'm not His masterpiece. I'm His practice piece.* They look at the woman sitting next to them, who seems to have it all, and they think, *She's the one who is His masterpiece.*

Yet we all come into this world in the same way—sinners, trying to paint our own canvas. And when we make a wrong choice in our life, a bad brush stroke appears. And we try to hide it or cover it up or make it blend into the overall picture of our lives. And then we make a *big* mistake, which ends up looking like a spill of paint right through the middle of the canvas. No matter what we do, we continue to mess up the painting every step of the way until we get to the point where we feel that *nothing* can salvage the creation.

That's when God, the Master Artist, patiently asks, "Are you finished yet? Will you give Me the brush and let Me do what only I can do with your life?" Sometimes we hesitate, thinking He will ask something of us that we don't want to do, or He'll take a dream from us and leave us miserable. Yet He's the One with the master plan of what our lives should look like. He's the One who created us in the first place and has been waiting to carry out His plan, if we would only surrender and hand the paintbrush over to Him.

When we finally, unreservedly hand Him the brush and admit that we truly need Him and His redeeming, restoring hand, it is amazing what happens next. He has a way of turning that painting upside down and inside out and recreating it in such a way that we are left saying, "How could He have made *this* with something like *that?*" And we end up wondering why we didn't hand Him that brush and our canvas long ago.

Second Corinthians 5:17 says, "What this means is that those who become Christians become new persons. They are not the same anymore, for the old life is gone. A new life has begun!" (NLT).

Kelly Morgan is a testimony of a new life that has begun. *You* can be, too!

Ways You Are Unique

One of the amazing ways that God recreates our canvas is that He doesn't completely remove those bad brush strokes, the consequences of our wrong choices that we believe have marred our masterpiece. Instead, our mistakes sometimes become part of the masterpiece. In His incredible way of redeeming the picture, God doesn't remove certain consequences from our life, but makes them work toward the beauty of it. A mistake in your past may make up the threads of your ministry today. Some pain from your childhood may be the pivotal point of how you reach out and extend to others today. Certain circumstances that you felt were unfortunate may be the catalysts for the degree of compassion you have today for others who have endured the same thing.

For you to fully appreciate who you are, where you've been, and how God can redeem it all, let's look at what makes you unique and how God can work through your circumstances.

Your Talents and Abilities—What is it that you do really well? This might be a skill you've learned, or an ability that came completely naturally. I mentioned in the first chapter that my older sister could pick up any instrument and play it from the time she was five years old. That was a huge key to her dream, but she had no idea at the time. What do *you* do well that seems to set you apart from others?

Your Upbringing—What is unique about how or where you were brought up? My cousin's wife, Yuliya, was raised in Russia and underwent persecution as a Christian. In coming to America, her heart beats to share the gospel of Christ with others in a country where she can freely speak it and people can freely live it. Her unique calling, I believe, is to be a witness for Christ to everyone she encounters. And you know what? She *loves* telling others about Jesus. Her dream was partly shaped by where she lived and how she grew up. What about *you*? Did you have some unique experiences as a child that might be linked to your dream today?

Your Mistakes or Lessons Learned—I know several women who were teenage single moms. Today they have not only a heart for but a ministry to other teens in the same situation. What did you

> *God delights in taking the unworkable or unworthy and making it completely worthy and of utmost value.*

have to learn the hard way so that others can be spared from making the same mistakes? That could be closely connected with your purpose. Maybe you were raised around drug or alcohol addicts or you experienced the ravages of divorce in your family or your marriage. Whatever you have gone through, and learned from, is another building block toward your purpose and your impact on the lives of others. It's the way God takes all things—even the bad things—and works them together for good to those who love Him (Romans 8:28).

Handing Over the Canvas

Who would've thought that a holy and perfect God would specialize—and delight—in taking messed-up paintings and making them into uniquely beautiful masterpieces? Yet that's what is called redemption. Restoration. And it's what God does best. Sadly, most of us don't discover the dream God has for us until our painting looks beyond repair. But nothing is beyond the saving, redeeming, restoring hand of God. He actually delights in taking the unworkable or unworthy and making it completely worthy and of utmost value.

Won't you hand Him the canvas of *your* life?

A Recreated "Canvas"

Bathsheba is a woman who really messed up. We know her as the woman whom King David lusted after and whom David committed adultery with. By the time the dust had settled, her husband had been murdered, and the child conceived in adultery had died. From then on, David's family had a history of problems. Yet at some point, Bathsheba handed over to God her torn and tattered canvas and allowed God to make her new. After all, it was her son, Solomon, who was selected to sit on the throne of Israel, even though he was not the eldest son, and therefore was not entitled to that throne at the time of David's death. But David wanted a man on the throne who would love God with all his heart. And David saw that heart in the son of Bathsheba.

It's doubtful David spent a lot of time with Solomon, considering he had a kingdom to run, and many wives, concubines, and children to tend to. So Bathsheba must have been the one to raise this wise and gentle son who had a desire to please God. Probably the ultimate honor and blessing in Bathsheba's life was that her name is listed in the genealogy of Christ—she is an ancestress of the Messiah. Interestingly enough, only four women's names are listed in the New Testament records of the ancestors of Jesus. And every one of them was a woman with a "marred canvas." Listed are Tamar, who disguised herself as a prostitue in order to conceive a child with her father-in-law; Rahab, who was a prostitute; Ruth, who was of the wicked Moabite culture; and Bathsheba. I believe God was making a point. It's never too late to become a blessing...and to leave a legacy. Not when you've got a Master Artist redesigning your canvas.

What About You?

Is it too late for you to be able to grab hold of a dream and blessing? Absolutely not! Take confidence from the fact that God put it in His Word in black and white that neither the desperate woman, nor the prostitute, nor the woman with the bad upbringing, nor the adulteress were excluded from His blessings.

They were women renewed, women redeemed, women restored. They were His poems. And His poems remain throughout history, standing the test of time.

Ask God to show you how *you* are His poem. His answer just might take your breath away.

~ *Dream On* ~

Let's explore a little further this whole idea of how you are God's unique expression of who He is. Answer the following questions thoughtfully and prayerfully:

1. What talents and abilities do you have that others seem to appreciate?

2. Can you think of something you can do that few others can? If so, what?

3. What do you think your spiritual gift might be? (A spiritual gift is an ability that you are able to carry out only through the power of God's Holy Spirit, and is used to build up the body of Christ, the church.) For a list of the spiritual gifts, see Romans 12:6-8, 1 Corinthians 12:7-11, and 1 Peter 4:10-11.

4. What is unusual about your upbringing, culture, experiences, or training?

5. What negative circumstances in your life might contribute to your uniqueness and your ability to minister to others?

6. In light of what you've learned, would you like to revise the dream concept you developed in earlier chapters? If so rewrite it here, incorporating any new insights you gained through this chapter.

~ *Press On* ~

How wonderful that when we are "in Christ" we are a new creation! And all of the mistakes we've made and the setbacks we've experienced can actually add to the uniqueness of who we are and how we can be used for God's glory. Ask your heavenly Father, my friend, to confirm to you the beauty that He sees when He looks at you through the image of His precious Son. You truly are a masterpiece…created to resonate with the glory of God's image stamped on you!

"Delight yourself in the LORD and he will give you the desires of your heart."

—PSALM 37:4

"He stood me up on a wide-open field; I stood there saved—surprised to be loved!"

—PSALM 18:19 (MSG)

4

Developing an Obedient Heart

*P*eggy never wanted to be a missionary. Like most of us, she figured that was someone else's calling. It certainly wasn't her dream—or so she thought.

So when she was asked to pray about joining her girlfriend on a missions trip to Russia, she simply refused to open the door to God.

"I wouldn't even pray about it," Peggy recalls. "I said, 'No, I'm too busy. I'll pray for *you* to go, but I just don't have the time to go.'"

When Peggy's friend returned from Russia, Peggy listened to her friend's exciting stories. Shortly afterward Peggy received a letter from a church sponsoring another trip to Russia. One phrase cut through her heart: *Have you ever asked God if He wanted you in Russia?*

She realized she had refused to ask God the question. So, desiring to be obedient, she told God she was willing to go to Russia if He wanted her to.

"I figured as long as I was willing to go, that was all God wanted. He wouldn't actually *send* me there."

She filled out her application and even went through the motions of getting funds for her trip, convinced God would pull her off the mission at the last moment. When the plane that was to take her out of the United States was delayed four hours, she was sure it was because God didn't want her to go, and was working to get her off the plane somehow.

But God saw Peggy through, all the way to Russia. As she traveled, her heart stirred within her. Why would God want her to venture into this territory she knew nothing about? Yet, she couldn't help but feel that *something* awaited her there. By the time she got off the train, which had transported her to her destination in Saransk, Peggy knew what that something was. It was the dream God had whispered on her heart.

"I ended up living a dream I never even realized I had," Peggy says now, four years after being obedient to the call on her heart to go to Russia.

"People ask me how long I've wanted to be a missionary," Peggy says. "I never knew I did. I supported missionaries. I prayed for missionaries. I've had missionaries in my home for dinner. But it was never a thought for *me* to be a missionary—and especially in Russia!"

Rather than setting out to pursue her dream, Peggy simply followed God in obedience. She sensed He wanted her to be willing to do whatever He asked. How could she have known that what God had asked her to do was what she had been called to do, but never knew it? Perhaps that's why God blessed in the way He did.

Peggy now returns to Russia once or twice a year. She feels fully alive as she goes back year after year, being reunited with men and women who have given their lives to Christ because

Peggy and others explained to them the gospel of Jesus through an interpreter.

Peggy now realizes she could've easily missed the dream had she not been willing to answer God's call to "go."

Moses of the Old Testament could have missed *his* call, too. And a whole nation of people would have paid the price. God called Moses to lead His people out of Egypt and Moses' response was, after several excuses, "O Lord, please send *someone else* to do it."[1] But God had already chosen whom He wanted for the job.

No One but Jonah

God also called Jonah to do some evangelistic work. "Get up and go to Nineveh," He told Jonah. God wanted Jonah to preach against this wicked city so it would repent. But Jonah didn't want to go, so he boarded a ship bound for Tarsus. Do you realize that God could've used *anyone* to go to Nineveh and preach repentance to the pagans? And when Jonah refused and boarded a ship in the opposite direction, it seems likely that God would've simply told another one of His prophets to go instead. But God apparently wanted Jonah for the job. And He wasn't about to go to "Plan B."

God was so determined that Jonah do the job that He hunted him down, sent a storm after him, had him cast into the sea, and then appointed (and perhaps even created, for this purpose only) a huge fish to swallow him to save him from drowning. God then had the fish regurgitate Jonah onto some shore and then gave him a second chance to "go."

After the bad fish experience, Jonah went. But he went reluctantly. And he did an awful job, too. Read the story. Jonah preached, but halfheartedly, with no passion whatsoever. He simply followed God's orders because he knew he would be busted again if he didn't. Yet God, in His grace, caused Jonah to succeed in his task and the people of Nineveh repented and were spared. (That's what Jonah didn't want to happen, by the way, which is probably why he did his job so halfheartedly.)

Jonah then had so much of an attitude that he went out to pout. The weather was hot and he was miserable, so God miraculously grew a plant to put shade over Jonah's head. Then to teach his hot-headed servant a lesson, God caused a worm to eat the plant so that it withered and died. This made Jonah upset. God then told him, in essence, "Why are you so concerned about this plant when you didn't create it and cause it to grow, yet you think nothing of the more than 120,000 people who would've died in their sins, not to mention all their animals?"

I wonder if Jonah ever got it.

I also wonder how the story would have played out differently if Jonah said yes to the original call. What if he saw God's call for him as a desirable plan? What if he trusted that what God wanted of his life was really what he wanted, too? I imagine Jonah would've found joy...and discovered his purpose. Who knows what other evangelistic missions God might have sent him on? But Jonah never found it. He grudgingly obeyed God and missed out on the blessing of a willing heart.

It's apparent God had a dream for Jonah to be a great prophet and help save the people of Nineveh. But Jonah was too wrapped up in himself to pursue what God wanted. It's clear he missed the blessings. What joy he could've experienced if he had just embraced what God had intended for him!

It's clear from Scripture that Jonah's assignment was just as much about the formation and development of Jonah's heart as it was about the task God wanted done. And I believe God sends things *our* way today to not only test our willingness to be faithful in the little things, but also to lead us a step closer toward our dream.

What does God want to do in and through your heart? And what would happen if you determined to enjoy the process?

Present-Day Jonahs

I guess I'm a Jonah, too. A year ago, a good friend of mine at my church asked me to go through some training in evangelism so I could not only share my faith more boldly, but teach others to do the same. As the director of women's ministries at my church, as well as an author and a Bible teacher, I was entrenched in discipleship—helping Christians grow in their faith. But I had little experience in evangelism—helping women, one on one, grasp the truth of God's plan of salvation for their lives.

"Soul winning is the first step in discipleship," Paul told me, as I stressed that my role was primarily to disciple women. I knew Paul was trying to tell me my spiritual life was out of balance. And I knew he was right. But like Jonah, I ran.

I rationalized: "But I'm a disciple-maker, not an evangelist."

"God commands you to do both," Paul replied.

Then I justified: "But I do speak boldly of my faith in my writing and speaking."

"But do you speak boldly to the woman in line at the grocery store?" Paul persisted.

I even spiritualized: "But I don't have the gift of evangelism."

"You're right," Paul replied. 'It's not your gift. It's your *command*."

Eventually my excuses wore thin. But let me tell you, I was scared to death to go to the laundromat with Paul and speak to strangers about my faith. I was desperately looking for the next ship to Tarsus. Then God got the message to me loud and clear.

I was speaking at a women's retreat and ended the last session with a call to the women to leave their baggage on shore and get into the boat with Jesus and go with Him to the other side. "Where does Jesus want to take you that you haven't been?" I asked the women as they came forward, crying, kneeling, and surrendering their reservations to Him. "What new place does He want to take you in your faith? Are you ready to go with Him to a new level—a new level of faith and trust and surrender? Then lay down your reservations and go. Leave your comfort zone and go. Be willing to go where *He* wants for a change."

Then conviction hit my heart—hard! I was making a challenge to these women that I wasn't willing to answer myself. I knew where God wanted to take me…He wanted me to leave my reservations about evangelism and go with Him to a new place of trust and faith and surrender. He wanted to stretch me and grow me and I had to leave my comfort zone in order to get into the boat with Jesus and go to the other side with Him. I knew I could not stand there asking women to go to a place where I wasn't willing to go. I knelt down, along with those women who came forward, to surrender and pray, and I knew by the time I got up that there was no going back.

I started the training and within three weeks had the privilege of sharing the gospel, one on one, with a woman and holding her hands and hearing her precious prayer of surrender. I witnessed hardened hearts soften. I saw God "show up" in homes where I was pretty sure He wouldn't have darkened the door. I saw a woman who thought she was unloved grasp the wonder of God's love for her and surrender her life to Jesus. In those 13 weeks of training, and yes—even visiting the laundromat—I not only experienced the joy that comes from sharing my faith boldly, but I can honestly tell you, I had the time of my life!

I realize now that I could've very easily gone into that assignment reluc-

> *When it comes to the call God places on our lives, He knows what He's doing. He knows who He wants for the job.*

tantly, like Jonah, and missed the blessing. But by asking God to give me a burning desire for His will, over my own, He was not only faithful in doing so, but caused me to *love* the assignment. Looking back now, I wonder how many of us miss blessings because we fear that when God calls us to do something, we'll be miserable. It also makes me wonder just how many followers of Christ are missing wonderful blessings simply because they still believe the lie that sharing the greatest news that exists is scary to do, will not be well-received, and reaps little results.

When it comes to the call God places on our lives, He knows what He's doing. He knows *whom* He wants for the job. The only problem is, sometimes we don't want the job. Yet it's God's dream, remember? And blessings will follow only if we are first obedient.

My dream was not to go out and evangelize. But by obediently following God's call, I finally arrived at the point of absolute surrender so I can be used by Him anytime and anywhere. God was taking me to the next step in fulfilling His dream for me. And today, knowing how to share the plan of salvation simply and confidently helps me in every area of living out my dream. If I limited my dream to merely writing books, I'd be limiting myself to just what I think I can do. Rather, God wants me to trust Him for *all* the things that *He* can do.

What Are You Missing?

If I had insisted on doing only what I wanted to do, I would have missed out on the immense joy of seeing people give their lives to Christ. If Peggy had insisted on living within the realm of what she could imagine, she would have missed the joys of seeing Russian men, women, and children come to Christ. But doesn't our Creator know better than we do what it is that will bring blessing into our lives…and what it is we'd ultimately love to do?

Jesus told His followers, "Seek first his kingdom and his righteousness, and all these things [including the dream, I believe] will be given to you as well" (Matthew 6:33).

I saw that played out in Peggy's life. She wanted God's will first—and in His love and grace, God gave Peggy her dream along with it.

So what are we afraid of? I remember thinking, at 22 years old, that if I recommitted my life to God and what He wanted for me, instead of what I wanted for myself, that He'd make me marry a pastor. And I did NOT want to be a pastor's wife. Yet shortly after recommitting my life to Him, and asking for a heart that loves Him alone, He brought into my life a man who loved God more than anyone I knew. And that man was studying to be a pastor! I see today, that through my marriage to a pastor, I gained the life and ministry experiences necessary to discover and live out my dream of writing for women. However, there were times when I wondered if I would *ever* be able to live out the dream on my heart.

Stumbling Through the Journey

As a young pastor's wife, I wanted to start out writing books immediately. So four years after marrying, I left my career job as a newspaper reporter, had a baby, and became a full-time mother. I figured my dream was right around the corner. I could stay home with the baby and write books all day. But God wanted to see, first, if I had a heart to obey Him and serve Him—wherever He might lead. (Looking back, marrying the pastor wasn't the test. After all, I was in love. Marrying him was easy. It was being obedient during the wait for the dream to arrive that was the *real* test for me.)

As the new pastor's wife, several people in the congregation made it their goal to see to it that I had a "place of service" in the church. So I was asked, first, to be a greeter at the church doors every Sunday morning. But that became impossible when I had my baby daughter clinging to my legs all the time. Then I was asked to help prepare communion for the worship service once a month. That was tolerable. But eventually, that became difficult when baby Dana began to toddle around the kitchen under my feet as I was trying to perform that simple task. By the time my daughter was barely two years old, I was asked to teach the twos and threes Sunday school class, which I soon realized was not the job cut out for me. A couple years later, my husband needed me to be his co-worship leader in a church that was literally bereft of musical talent. In all that time, I served at those various positions waiting on God for the place of service that would truly make my heart sing. Then finally, I was asked to lead a monthly women's Bible study at the church. Now *there* was a task I enjoyed doing! I enjoyed it so much I began writing the studies I taught, and I began to see God develop in me a heart to study His Word and teach it to women.

Just about the time I'd found my niche in writing and teaching studies for women at my church, I was asked to do another something I wasn't that good at. Our church was hosting a missions conference and my husband asked that I make Sunday dinner for some visiting missionaries. Now, everyone who knows me knows I don't cook particularly well. And I don't enjoy cooking, either. I am blessed with a husband who enjoys creating menus and cooking, so I usually try to be a support to him by setting the table and "heating up" side dishes! But back when I still thought I cooked pretty well, I agreed to open our home to these missionaries and cook a meal for them. Now this was around the time that I was very frustrated about wanting to live my dream of writing and speaking, but was being put into jobs that just weren't me. I was doing things I *could* do, but not the things that made my heart sing. And I just kept wondering, *When is God going to release me to live my dream?* Well, around the table that afternoon, one of the missionaries happened to ask, "Cindi, what do you like to do? What's your ministry?" (And I'm sure he was hoping I wouldn't say, "I love to cook for people.")

I responded, "I love writing and teaching Bible studies and my dream is to write books for women out of the studies I've taught." And, to my surprise, this missionary said, "My son-in-law is an editor at a Christian publishing house. You should send your book ideas to him." Well, I did. And although what I had written was not what that publishing house was looking for at the time, that particular editor happened to remember my name on my return address label when I sent an unsolicited book proposal to him two years later. And for some reason, that unsolicited material ended up on his desk, he read through it, and gave me a call, saying that he remembered me and he believed I had something the publishing house was interested in. And that was the open door to the publishing house that I've had all my books published with. What's more, that same editor has become a good friend who has continued to present my ideas to the publishing committee for approval, and is still editing my books today.

I find it interesting that my connection into publishing ultimately happened through engaging in an activity I least liked (cooking). Yet looking back, I can see clearly that God opened the door to my dream as a result of my obedience. It's possible God is waiting in a similar way for *you*, too.

What About You?

What might God be calling you to do that you really don't want to do at all? Are you, like Moses, thinking, *Please, God, send somebody else*? Where is He calling you to go that doesn't seem likely will lead to anything related to your dream? Are you like Jonah, knowing clearly what God wants you to do but not wanting to do it, or just not thinking you have it in you to accomplish it? Well you don't. He's waiting to accomplish it in and through you! And He's waiting to reward you for your leap of faith and your heart of surrender.

How do you need to surrender in order to get one step closer to living out your dream?

Surrender Your Plans—Get in the practice of telling God, "Not my will, but Yours." We often have our own image of what the dream will look like, how we'll get it, and when. Yet Proverbs 16:3 says, "Commit your works to the LORD and your plans will be established." It doesn't say plan out your way, move full speed ahead, and expect God to follow. The verse says to commit your works to Him. Hold them with an open hand and say, as Jesus said to His heavenly Father in the Garden as He suffered over not wanting to do what He ultimately had to do, "Not my will, but Yours be done." God honored His Son's prayer. And He will honor your prayer as well, once He knows that what you ultimately want is what He wants for you. That's the kind of heart we need to have before we can truly live out our dream. Remember Bonnie in chapter 2? She wanted to teach dance in order to help women find their worth. But she had to surrender to the fact that God might want her to do that in another form, like speaking or writing. Being flexible to God's plans and not insisting on our own, is key to living out the dream He intended.

Surrender Your Fears—Often it's the fear and doubt that holds us back from being able to pursue and live out our dream. Yet there is a freedom that comes with trusting God, in spite of the obstacles.

> *Remember, it's all about Him, and not about us.*

My friend, Marilyn, who always wanted to speak and write, said she found peace in her heart when she let go of the question of how God was going to overcome all her obstacles and she simply started trusting Him by obeying what He told her to do each day. For Marilyn, surrendering her fear of not being able to reach or live out her dream is a day-by-day, step-by-step process.

Surrender Your Ego—John the Baptist was a prophet on the rise in his day. People came from miles around to see this guy and hear him speak. He would surely be a sell-out speaker if the culture were like ours today. Yet John knew Jesus, his cousin, was in town. He could've viewed Jesus as competition. But Jesus was the coming Messiah…the reason for which John had a ministry and message. And John's words epitomize the essence of humility: "He must increase, but I must decrease" (John 3:30 NASB). In another translation, John's words are, "He must become greater; I must become less." If that is truly *our* motto, God will know that we can indeed handle the dream He wants to assign us because we'll be ever aware that He is the source and the fuel behind it. Remember, it's all about Him, and not about us.

True Blessings Will Follow

Does all this seem like too much? To surrender our plans, our fears, *and* our egos? God says to obey is better than sacrifice (1 Samuel 15:22). Better than promising God one-tenth of all your fortunes if He gives you the dream, better than committing to be in church every Sunday if He just lets you live out your dream, better than any promise, commitment, or sacrifice you can think of is the simple task of obeying God with all your heart. The true sacrifices of God are a broken heart (or will) and contrite spirit (Psalm 51:17). That means to be crushed…and moldable… and surrendered to Him in *every* way.

It is then that the true blessings follow.

Dream On

Holding yourself back when God is asking you to step forward will restrict you. Yet when you let go and release to Him the reins of your life, you'll enjoy the most freeing and liberating state you've ever experienced.

First John 4:18 says perfect love casts out fear. To love God perfectly is to trust Him completely. And when we trust Him completely, there is no room for fear. Do you love Him that much? Enough to trust Him with the unknown? If so, you're finally ready to pursue your dream.

Think through the following questions as a way of discovering what might still be holding you back, and wherein lies the key to finally moving forward:

1. What has God asked you to do recently that you haven't yet done?

    (It might not seem like the task is connected to your dream, but if it's a matter of obedience, it surely is. Write here a prayer to God, surrendering your will to His and vowing to do what you know He's been asking you to do.)

2. Which area of surrender is the most difficult for you, and why?

- Surrendering your plans
- Surrendering your fears
- Surrendering your ego

3. Read the following verses and record one of the blessings that come from obedience. Think about how this relates to your dream as well.

John 15:10-11

1 John 2:5

Psalm 1:1-3

Psalm 32:6-8,11

Psalm 34:15

Psalm 34:17

Psalm 34:18

Psalm 34:19

Proverbs 3:5-6

Isaiah 30:18

Isaiah 48:17-18

～ *Press On* ～

Think about it. Your single act of obedience in an area in which you might be hesitating could be the step toward a contact or opportunity you know nothing about. Sometimes the connections we arrange on our own—which we think will usher us toward our dream—actually leave us lingering still in the desert. And the ones we think have nothing to do with our dream are the ones that could fling the doors wide open. That's how God works; He's full of surprises. You, too, could find yourself saying, as the psalmist did in Psalm 118:25:

> "This is GOD's work. We rub our eyes—we can hardly believe it! This is the very day GOD acted—let's celebrate and be festive! Salvation now, God. Salvation now! Oh yes God—a free and full life!" (MSG).

Part II

*Pursuing
the
Dream*

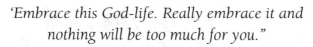

'Embrace this God-life. Really embrace it and
nothing will be too much for you."

—MARK 11:22 (MSG)

5

Being a "Big Dream" Believer

When Lori began studying broadcast journalism at the suggestion of a college guidance counselor, she had no idea of the heartache that lay ahead. "It never occurred to me that you had to be beautiful to make it in this business," she said. Petite, with a nice smile and warm brown eyes, Lori went on, "I got my first clue after a summer internship. The coordinator said, 'You're no Miss America, so you'll have to work very hard.'" Lori admits that, at 20 years of age, that was good advice. And work hard she did.

Lori liked reporting and anchoring not because she liked seeing herself on the air, but because it afforded her the opportunity to meet a lot of people and it combined many skills she enjoyed: public speaking, writing, video production. But the field was quite competitive. "Once I was told the job was almost mine but the woman chosen was selected for 'obvious cosmetic reasons.' I got rejection letters that said 'your talents don't fit our needs.' I figured I just didn't fit." One colleague told her she would never make it very far in the business if she didn't lose weight. A news director told her, "You've gained weight since your audition. You need to watch your size."

Discouraged, but determined to not give up, Lori found a job where her behind-the-camera skills were appreciated and she even got to anchor once in a while and report as often as she wanted. But then the company hit hard times. To keep her job, she willingly moved to a position that bored and depressed her. It wasn't challenging, and it didn't make her heart sing.

"I missed reporting the news," Lori recalls. "And I figured I was too wrinkly and too out of touch to get a job in a newsroom ever again."

About that time, some friends of hers were working for a faith-based network. She went to see one of them to inquire about contacts and job possibilities. An acquaintance found out where Lori was inquiring and said, "You'll *never* get a job there." The day of her appointment, Lori sat in the lobby, alone, beneath a large cross on the wall. She looked up at that cross and prayed, "God, I'd love to work here, but only if You want me to." The prayer was not just an expression of the desire of her heart, but a prayer of surrender. She really wanted God's will for her life more than her own.

The next week Lori received a call from her friend at the faith-based organization.

"We're starting a news department and we want you to be the news director," her future boss said. "Oh, and you'll be the daily anchor. We reach 32 million people nationwide."

"Wow," Lori recalls. "To work in a news department again. To work for a Christian-based network. And they wanted me to anchor! Wasn't I too old? Too fat? Too Un-Miss America? Guess not."

Lori took that job. And today, she is living her dream.

"When God gives us our dream. He gives it all the way," Lori told me recently. Her dream was to communicate current events in a responsible way, and that's what she's doing today.

Lori laughs, too, at how God reminded her recently of the obstacles He overcame on her behalf to land her in this dream job.

"The other day, I heard my boss say, 'We hired Lori for her looks!' God not only gives us a dream; He has a sense of humor," she said.

The hard road toward realizing her dream has kept Lori humble in a career field where one could easily become prideful. She remembers, every day, that it was God who made her dream a reality once she surrendered to Him at the foot of the cross. Today she's grateful that she didn't back down when others told her she didn't have what it takes. And she never gave up on the dream…or the One who held it in His hands, waiting to give it to her.

⚮

Can you relate to Lori's story? Have you, too, been told your dream was unrealistic or too far-fetched? Has anyone ever implied that you have been shooting too far above what you're capable of or what's possible?

"Who am I to think God would have something big planned for me?" You've either heard those words or said them to yourself, haven't you? Perhaps we need to remember, like Lori did, that we have a God who knows the desires of our hearts. And if there's a big dream on our hearts, it's very possible that a Big God put it there and plans to hand it to us to remind us just how big He is.

Unlikely "Fits"

Throughout the Bible I find people who might have believed they weren't a likely fit for what God wanted to do with their lives. Perhaps they even believed the big dream was a bit too big for them.

When Queen Esther was approached by her cousin Mordecai to plead before King Ahasuerus for the lives of the Jewish people under the king's rule to be spared, she believed it was an assignment she wasn't capable of. "But it's been a month since I've been called before the king. And if I go to him without being summoned, I could die for it." She was, in a sense, saying, "Who am I to save my people? I'm a woman with no power of my own. I can't do anything." Yet her conscience was pricked when her cousin asked the convicting question: "Who knows but that you have come to [your] royal position for such a time as this?" (Esther 4:14). In other words, "Don't you think there's a reason you are in the position you are in at this point in time? There's a greater purpose at work here. Don't miss it!" When Esther agreed to put herself in the position where God could work through her, she accomplished an amazing feat. She became known throughout biblical and Jewish history as "the queen who saved her people."

∽◯

What if Miriam, Moses' sister, had gotten tired of living in the shadow of her famous brother and decided she would not lead the Israelite nation in song after crossing the Red Sea?

"Moses, Moses, Moses…it's all about Moses," she could've complained. "Get him to do the job. Everyone likes him better anyway. Nobody even knows who I am."

What if she had hesitated because she didn't like to be in front of people? What if she had rationalized that she was too dysfunctional to be used for God's purposes because of the horrors she saw while growing up in Egypt? Yet Miriam, who is called a prophetess in the Bible, stepped out and became an instant national worship leader—all because she was willing and available to let a Big God do something bigger in and through her life.

✺

I'm so glad Joseph didn't hesitate or fail to believe in a Big God when God gave him his big dream. It's interesting how God, through two dreams, revealed to Joseph that he would rule over his older brothers, as well as his parents.

Though Joseph didn't understand what his dreams meant, he didn't question God about them. But others certainly questioned Joseph. His father rebuked him for having a dream that implied his whole family would bow to him some day. His brothers couldn't fathom that God would raise up their younger brother to rule over them. I've often thought Joseph was unusually bold to mention his dreams to his brothers and father. By telling his family his dreams, he appears to be outright bragging, even though he wasn't. What did he expect their reaction might be?

Joseph had a tremendous amount of faith to be so bold in telling others his dreams.

With every big dream comes testing, trying, and trusting.

Rather than questioning God's revelation that one day he would be lifted up as a leader, Joseph must have readily accepted that he had a Big God who could do such a big work in his life. He trusted God regarding the dreams, but he had no idea what he'd have to go through before the dreams were fulfilled.

Look at Joseph's Experience

With every big dream comes testing, trying, and trusting. It's been said that nothing in life that's really worth it comes easily. Well, Joseph's realization of God's plans for him is a perfect example of this. It's possible that at times Joseph wished he'd never had the dreams at all. Or that God had chosen someone else for the job. Yet Joseph remained faithful for years. And it took that long for God to develop him into the kind of leader he needed to be to finally live out the big dream.

The Testing—Joseph's first big test, I imagine, is how he handled the wounds associated with proclaiming his dream to others. When his father rebuked him and his brothers resented him, he didn't go back to God and say, "Forget it, God. Choose someone else. If I follow You, I'll lose everyone close to me." Joseph must have had a dedication to God that went deeper than his dedication to his family. Could you pass that kind of test? If you, like Peggy in chapter 3, were called to go to Russia and share the gospel, would you back out of the call if your friends and family disapproved? If you are convinced you need to return to school at this point in life and begin pursuing a career, would you give up if people around you said, "That's crazy"?

There have been times when my travel schedule gets hectic, most often after the release of a new book. I remember thinking several times that I was letting people down by being gone a lot. I had to call in substitute teachers for my Bible class, have an assistant lead my discipleship group, reschedule appointments with others, and take the risk of looking unreliable at times. The people-pleasing instinct within me wants to accommodate everyone, and my tendency toward pride shudders at what others might think of me when I let them down. Yet my obedience to God, and what He's calling me to do, *must* be more important than others' reactions to what I do. I don't *always* pass the test with flying colors, and I still feel regret when I have to reschedule someone or let someone down, but I realize that's the test that's always in front of me: Whom would I rather disappoint? God or others?

After Joseph passed his people-pleasing tests, the tests got a bit more severe. I refer to his severe testing as a *trying* process because of the long wait that was involved.

The Trying—Joseph was sold into slavery. But because Joseph kept a right heart, God prospered him and made him head of the household where he served. Then Joseph was imprisoned for three years on false charges. But because he kept a right heart, God continued to prosper him and made him overseer of all who were with him in prison. Then Joseph was promised release for interpreting a dream, but he was forgotten for another couple years. Joseph could've become bitter about doing the right thing and being repeatedly tried and tested as a result. Yet Joseph remained faithful to God. He appears to have had a quiet trust in the Almighty. Apparently, Joseph chose to trust that the Dream Giver knew what He was doing.

The Trusting—Because Joseph kept a right heart during the trying and the waiting and the injustice he endured, God saw that he was ready to accept the Big Assignment and live out the dream. God saw that Joseph could serve as a leader while being a slave in his master's house and while being an inmate in prison. As Joseph trusted God with the trying and testing, he was being shaped into the man he needed to be to lead all of Egypt. It's possible that as God saw Joseph hold no bitterness toward those who wronged him, He also saw that Joseph would deal rightfully with his brothers when the family was eventually reunited in Egypt. Joseph's trust in God every step of the way built into him a humility he would need later. When Joseph finally met his brothers, he extended grace, rather than wanting to get even. He'd grown into a man who wasn't concerned about retribution, but reconciliation and forgiveness. (This story is found in Genesis 37, 39—46.) Only humility can do that to us, especially when we've been exalted to a place where we're living out our dream. And God knows that we gain the humility we need to live out our Big Dream when we've been through the testing, trying, and trusting phases.

Getting Ready for the Dream

How can you be prepared to "go" when God says "go" in terms of a Big Dream for your life?

Listen to Your Convictions

All it took was a couple dreams for Joseph to realize God wanted to do something bigger with his life. For some of us, though, we have to be brought to a point of conviction. We learn of a source of injustice or we become burdened over a matter that we know burdens God's heart, and we feel strongly that we must respond. That's the way it was with Nehemiah in the Bible. He felt extremely burdened when he heard the wall around Jerusalem was in ruins after the desolation from Babylon. After spending much time in prayer, fasting, and tears, Nehemiah asked for God to grant him success in going before the king to ask for permission to rebuild the walls around Jerusalem. Nehemiah knew he was in a position where he could *do* something about the problem. And instead of saying "God, *should* I go?" his prayer was, "Be with me *as* I go." Perhaps the conviction on Nehemiah's heart was so strong that he knew better than to ask if he *should* go, and instead, asked for God's favor as he went.

Later, in Nehemiah 6:3, after others attempted to discourage Nehemiah and persuade him to stop the project, he replied by referring to what he was doing as a "great work." Nehemiah felt deeply concerned over a matter that burdened God's heart (the destruction of the walls around Jerusalem). And that's all it took for Nehemiah to step boldly into the Big Dream God had for his life.

Look At the Assignment

Queen Esther had to deal with the question, "Who knows but that you have come to [your] royal position for such a time as this?" Have you ever asked yourself that question in light of certain circumstances? Acknowledging that God is sovereign over all things helps us realize He is also able to appoint us for a certain task at a certain time. And responding to that could be key to stepping into our Big Dream.

God came right out and told Jeremiah, "Before I formed you in the womb I knew you, before you were born I set you apart; I appointed you as a prophet to the nations." Jeremiah's response sounds like fear: "Ah, sovereign LORD," he said. "I do not know how to speak; I am only a child." But God's response reminded Jeremiah who was in charge: "Do not say, 'I am only a child.' You must go to everyone I send you to and say whatever I command you. Do not be afraid of them, for I am with you and I will rescue you." I love what comes next: "Then the LORD reached out his hand and touched [Jeremiah's] mouth and said to [him], 'Now I have put my words in your mouth. See, today I appoint you over nations and kingdoms....'"[1] God called Jeremiah to a task and equipped him for that task. He didn't leave out any details. Again, God knew what He was doing and whom He was calling.

Frequently in the Old Testament, when God called someone to a Big Dream, their response was, "I can't do it." Moses said this. Jeremiah said this. Gideon said this. But every time, God reminded them that He knew them better than they knew themselves, and surely He wouldn't appoint them for the Big Assignment if He didn't intend to work through them to accomplish it. The Bible says God makes no mistakes. And that applies to the people He selects to carry out an assignment.

Learn to Go Where God Leads You

As you begin to take notice of what God is doing all around you, you will be more in tune with where God is leading you. And you won't want to miss it. Henry Blackaby, in his insightful study *Experiencing God*, encourages followers of God to look at where God is working and join Him there. How do you know where God is working? When God starts to do something out of the ordinary. For instance:

- When someone asks you about your faith. The Bible says that people, in general, are not interested in spiritual matters. So if someone's asking questions, God is at work in

her heart and bringing her to you for a divine appointment.

- When there's a need and you feel the pressing conviction
  that God is wanting to get the job done through you.

- When God confirms a matter to you through His Word,
  through circumstances in your life, or through the advice
  of a trusted Christian friend.

It's been said that some people have the "gift" of evangelism.
Yet in the Bible, sharing the gospel is not listed as a "gift." It is (as
my friend Paul reminded me) a command. Yet it seems there are
some Christians who are so good at sharing that it appears they
must be gifted in some way. My Aunt June is one of those people.
She can be walking down the street, be stopped by someone, and
the conversation will somehow end with her sharing the gospel
and the other person praying to receive Christ...right there on the
street.

Aunt June lives in the midst of divine appointments every day
of her life. I've had times when I've wondered if Aunt June has
something I don't. After all, we both love Jesus, and we are both
capable of the same works through the power of Christ within us.
But the more I talk with her, and the more I see her in action, the
more I'm convinced that the difference is that Aunt June has been
so faithful in what God has given her that He just keeps giving her
more. She's been faithful to not pass up an opportunity to share
the gospel of Christ with countless people. So God continues to
bring her way countless more people who need to hear about
God's saving grace. And He does this in extraordinary ways. To
this day, God continues to arrange divine appointments with
His lost sheep and my Aunt June because He knows His faithful

servant will do what she's commanded to help bring those sheep home.

∽∾

Are *you* going where God is leading? Are you looking for opportunities around you that could be divine appointments? Are you seeking to be a part of the plan that your Creator has for you? If so, God is taking note of your faithfulness, and He knows when you will be ready to be trusted with your Big Dream.

~ *Dream On* ~

1. Can you recall an area of testing and how this might be part of your preparation to live out your dream?

2. What are some "trying" times you've experienced as you've waited and trusted in God for Him to bring about deliverance or your dream?

3. In what ways have you learned to trust God so you can be better prepared to live out your dream?

4. James 4:10 says, "Humble yourselves before the Lord, and he will lift you up." In what ways have you learned humility so that you can better handle, without pride, the dream God wants to place in your hands?

~ Press On ~

How good it is to know that God sees us as far more capable of accomplishing certain things than we do. That's because He sees His power at work within us. And He knows that *He* can accomplish anything! In Ephesians 1:18-20, the apostle Paul prayed that Christians would know God's "incomparably great power" at work within us. The Greek word he used to speak of that power is equivalent to our English words *hyper mega dynamite* power. Do you realize, my friend, that God instills in you a kind of *hyper mega dynamite* power to accomplish that which He gives you to do? With that in mind, there really is nothing you can't accomplish through Christ's "incomparably great power" at work within you.

Now *that,* my friend, should make you a "big dream" believer once again!

*"The future belongs to those who believe in
the beauty of their dreams."*
—ELEANOR ROOSEVELT

*"God's Spirit beckons.
There are things to do and places to go!"*
—ROMANS 8:14 (MSG)

6

Launching the Dream

All her life, Sharil dreamed of being a nurse. Her heart stirred inside her when it came to the thought of helping people.

As a single mom with two children, she worked full time, fought the obstacles of a lack of money and a lack of resources and, at times, felt a lack of emotional support. But she stuck it out. Now married, with four children, Sharil is working on the finishing stages of becoming a registered nurse. The journey has taken her ten years. But it's not about to be over.

"My dream took on a different shape once I came to know God personally," she said. And now her dream is not to merely work as a nurse, but to open a board-and-care home for the elderly.

"I had a really great relationship with my grandmother," Sharil said. "She always wanted to open a board-and-care home. It was always a dream of hers. But she didn't have the education to do it or the know-how. I took care of her as she got older. She became my inspiration. I was working in a nursing home and getting to know all the elderly people and I learned so much about life there. They offered me so much history. It helped shape me and who I am. I have a lot of respect for older women in what they've seen and gone through and overcome."

But Sharil didn't like a lot of the places she saw that cared for the elderly. "There was never enough help. The food wasn't that great. People seemed to be just waiting to die."

That's when Sharil became determined to live out her dream.

"I realized these people have given so much to the world. Why can't I give back to them? It was time to give back…to God and to others."

While Sharil still has a ways to go to reach her dream of opening the board-and-care home, she has launched that dream and worked on it enough to know clearly where she is heading. She has managed to do the most difficult part for most of us: get started.

Now that you have a better idea of what your dream is (based on your basic dream concept and the questions you've worked through in each chapter), it's time to look at a process for getting started and seeing that dream become a reality.

Begin with the 3-D Approach

No matter what goal you are pursuing—whether it's writing a book, going back to school, starting a business, developing a ministry, or something else—you need a plan. I believe the upcoming 3-D approach will help you follow your dream. It's actually a prayer—a 3-D prayer that I prayed as I was determining to follow my dream and that I now pray for others as they begin to follow their dream as well. The three Ds are discernment, direction, and discipline. And this is how they can be incorporated into the pursuit of *your* dream:

Discernment—To discern something is to perceive a situation with insight and good judgment. One caution you want to heed is to not rush into what you believe is your dream and find out later it really isn't. Hopefully by now you've gained some insight about what your dream might be by asking questions such as, "What do I do really well?" and "What did I love to do as a child?" and "What do others perceive I have a knack for?" Those questions were all aimed at

> *God will often call us toward something that for awhile has been burning in our heart.*

giving you a certain amount of discernment so that you can know where God might be calling you.

Now, sometimes when we have a dream in mind, or a burden we feel we must pursue, or we're simply asked to do something, we have to figure out if it's what *we'd* like to do, or what *someone else* would like us to do, or if it's what *God* is calling us to do. We can determine the answer and gain discernment by asking:

1. *Is this something someone else can just as easily do?* If so, then maybe you're not necessarily being uniquely called to do it. All through our Christian lives, we will see opportunities to fulfill needs, and should help do so if we are able, along with fellow believers. Serving others should be a part of our lives, but such service won't necessarily be the same as a special calling. For example, Nehemiah (in chapter 5) knew he was the only one who was in a position to rebuild the ruined walls of Jerusalem.

2. *Is this something I have a strong heart's desire to do?* God generally calls us to a task we would enjoy doing, or that matches some of our natural abilities or areas of spiritual giftedness. And He'll often call us toward something that for awhile has been burning in our heart. Sharil wanted to be a nurse all her life. So the idea of opening a board-and-care home for the elderly is not just something she'd *like* to do, but something she feels God has given her a burden for.

3. *Is this something I feel God prodding me to do?* Sometimes that conviction in our hearts simply won't go away—the need is very apparent, and no one else is stepping forward to meet it. When that happens, lift the matter to the Lord in prayer. If the burden persists, then it may be God's special calling. That's probably how Nehemiah knew for sure that *he* was the man for the job! And it's probably how Sharil knows she is the one to fulfill this dream that she shared with her grandmother.

When we take these questions to the Lord and say, "God, please confirm to me if I am the one to do this" and then wait for His answer, we can be more certain that we are *called* to a specific task or ministry and we can have greater assurance that our dream is tested and true.

Direction—Since I've known all my life that I was to be a writer, for me the question was, "*What* am I supposed to write?" If your dream is to open a business, what kind of business should it be? Do your research. What is involved? What kind of permits do you need? Who else has done this and can give you helpful information? If you feel compelled to return to school, what should you study? Having a clear direction will keep you from working aimlessly toward nothing in particular. The key to direction is having a place to start and then a process to follow. I actually wrote out, step by step, my plan for beginning a book, my timeline for completing it, and my plan and schedule for submitting it to various publishers. Having a schedule and timeline not only kept me going, but gave me the feeling that I was being productive as I crossed items off my list of things to do. This also continually reminded me of where I needed to go next. If you know what it is that will motivate you to keep going, then incorporate that into your direction and your plan.

Discipline—Just do it! Many of us just don't take the time to do what it takes to get to our goal. After doing your research and coming up with a plan, give yourself a deadline. You can also set deadlines for each stage in the process. I outlined a year at a time what I could do to get closer to my dream. And I prayed daily for the discipline I needed and pushed myself to meet those deadlines and be able to cross a task off my list and see that I was getting closer to the goal.

Here is a set of guidelines for being disciplined:

1. Determine what it is that needs to be done.

2. Set a schedule for when you will do it. (For example: I will open the business by this date, which means I must accomplish these smaller tasks by these earlier dates.)

3. Do it—even when something else comes up. In terms of my writing, I paid my registration for a writer's conference, and then I pushed myself to have proposals ready by the

time of the conference. I put myself in a situation where I
had to be disciplined.

4. Have someone hold you accountable. Choose someone
who cares about you and believes enough in your dream
to get tough with you if you start to back away from it.

After working through the 3-D approach, I soon realized that
I needed to incorporate a fourth D:

Determination—Don't give up. Always have a next step. Each
time I got a rejection letter from a publisher, I made a point of
sending out another query letter the next day so there was always
a glimmer of hope out there somewhere. And at times the prayer
wasn't, "God, help it to get published." Instead, it was, "God,
please keep me hopeful. Keep something out there long enough
for me to still hold onto hope." God was always faithful to that
prayer. After all, He didn't want me to give up on the dream,
either.

∽

Finally, after following all that, believe it will happen. The
Bible says faith is "the assurance of things hoped for, the conviction of things not seen" (Hebrews 11:1 NASB). And a dream, for a
long time, is *not seen*. It exists only in our mind and heart. That's
when we need to trust that if God truly whispered that dream
into our hearts, He will bring it to pass in His own way and time.

To help with my determination, I had several God-confidence
verses that kept me going:

1. *Psalm 84:11*—"No good thing does he withhold from those
whose walk is blameless."

2. *Psalm 37:4-6*—"Delight yourself in the LORD and he will give you the desires of your heart. Commit your way to the LORD; trust in him and he will do this: He will make your righteousness shine like the dawn, the justice of your cause like the noonday sun."

3. *Psalm 37:7*—"Be still before the LORD and wait patiently for him; do not fret when men succeed in their ways [and you don't]...."

Perhaps the single most inspiring and confidence-building verses in my own life have been Psalm 18:28-29:

> You, O LORD, keep my lamp burning; my God turns my darkness into light. With your help I can advance against a troop; With my God I can scale a wall.

There were many times I needed God to keep my lamp of passion for the dream burning. And I needed Him to turn the darkness of despair into light and hope. I can count many times that He helped me run against a troop and leap over a wall.

What is *your* "troop" that you need God-confidence to go up against in order to follow your dream? Is it a troop of doubts, insecurities, lack of support from others? God is big enough to help you run upon it.

What is the wall you need to scale so that you can reach your dream? Is it a huge wall of money? Is it a wall of time? Is it a wall of intimidation or fear or doubt? Is it a wall of inconvenience or lack of discipline? Your God is big enough to help you leap over it.

You Have an Obligation

I remember when the wall of intimidation loomed over me. I had attended my first writer's conference and I realized how unprepared I was for the world of publishing. Getting a book published seemed so far away and so unattainable. But in the closing session, a woman who works as a writing agent stood up and practically yelled her encouragement at us. "You can do this," she said. "If God is truly calling you to be a writer, He'll make it happen no matter how discouraging your situation might seem right now." Then she said the words I'll never forget: "Only *you* can kill the dream God has placed in your heart."

I was determined, from that day forward, to not be the one responsible for letting my dream die. If God wanted to see this through in me, I'd be obedient to see it through for Him. You, too, have an obligation to the Dream Giver. Don't let Him down by giving up now.

~ *Dream On* ~

1. Practice your *discernment:* What is the dream you now feel ready to launch? Write a specific goal or two that you hope to accomplish.

2. Incorporate some *direction:* What is your plan? Write here how you will get started:

3. Apply the *discipline:* Write your strategy for accomplishing the above plan. (For example: What hour of the day will you work on it? How much time will you spend on it? And so on…)

4. Practice your *determination:* What are your God-confidence verses? Write them out here. (If you need some help, here are a few suggestions: Job 42:2; Psalm 18:28-29; Mark 11:24; Ephesians 3:20.) Commit to memory the verses that are most meaningful to you.

My God-Confidence Verses:

Press On

Count on God to keep your lamp burning and help you run upon that troop and leap over that wall. After all, He's the One who can part the seas, bring city walls down flat, change the hearts of kings, and raise a Savior from the dead. Surely there is nothing beyond His ability to do through you. Take heart, my friend. With the Dream Weaver being for you, you *can* bring to fulfillment the dream He has placed in your heart.

"Take a good look at me, God, my God; I want to look life in the eye, so no enemy can get the best of me or laugh when I fall on my face. I've thrown myself headlong into your arms—I'm celebrating your rescue. I'm singing at the top of my lungs, I'm so full of answered prayers."

—PSALM 13:3-6 (MSG)

7
Fighting for the Dream

*I*t took a major life crisis to help my sister, Kristi, discover her dream.

Throughout her life, she had toyed with a variety of careers, home-based businesses, and entrepreneurial ventures. But all to no avail. The purpose she was looking for couldn't be found in an inventive way to make some extra cash or something to pass the time away. She had a dream locked up in her heart that wouldn't be revealed until she was broken from the inside out.

At 38 years old, childhood issues that Kristi had never dealt with came crashing to the surface of her life. Suddenly she was faced with a complete disconnect between her logic and emotional processing ability.

"I was mentally and emotionally a child again, subconsciously trying to 'fix' all that had gone wrong in my childhood," she said. "It was difficult for me to discern between fiction and reality, and I ending up making a lot of bad choices during that time." But unaware of the real reasons behind her sudden shift in emotional stability, she blamed her husband. She tried leaving him several times and became convinced he was a parental image she had to get rid of in order to survive.

Kristi went to a series of Christian counselors who all told her the same advice (that she had issues from her childhood that she needed to deal with) and tried to help her understand why she was unable to process in an adult frame of mind.

"As a Christian, it was an absolutely devastating experience," Kristi said. "I cried out to God every day, praying He would fill me with what was missing and heal all the brokenness in my past. During this time I experienced depression, obsessive complusiveness, and self-destructive behavior. I had completely withdrawn. Many of my closest friends rejected me, and I was fearful that God would reject me as well. But the opposite was true. His arms were always reaching out, waiting for me to reach back."

Through everything that happened, Kristi's husband, Steve, never gave up on her. "Seeing his unconditional love helped me make the decision to reject how I *felt* and focus on what I *knew* to be the truth. I decided I was going to stay with Steve no matter what, and God would have to change my heart."

In counseling, Kristi was repeatedly encouraged to journal her thoughts. But no matter how she tried, she couldn't make sense of the words that would come out. "Spiritually I had hit the bottom and was looking up, waiting for anything to change the holding pattern I was in. That's when the music came.

"My thoughts turned into lyrics with melodies attached. God gave me a way to journal that touched the deepest part of my soul—through music."

Music had always been Kristi's passion. She was a music major in college and had started a new voice-teaching business in her home. But she didn't play the piano and never tried to write lyrics because she never had a reason or desire to do so.

"Suddenly music was my lifeline to God and recovery," she said. "I would wake up during the night with lyrics I couldn't shake. I couldn't drive without a notebook next to me so I could write the lyrics. And miraculously, I could play on the piano what was in my head. [Kristi had always had a knack for being able to play an instrument by ear.] After just a few weeks I had written nearly ten songs and was annoyed and a bit angry. This was becoming so time consuming I didn't want to do it anymore. I figured it would never amount to anything, so what was the point?"

Then God spoke to her clearly in her head, saying, "All you have to do is write them down."

"I promised God that if I was the only one to ever hear my music, then that was enough for me. God was clearly using this as a healing process in my life and it was worth the time involved—and it was cheaper than counseling!"

After a few months, the songs kept coming, and Kristi started to record them in her home studio. At Christmas that year she wrote a song for her husband, whom she refers to as "the most amazing man in the world to me now," and presented it to him as a gift under the tree Christmas morning.

"I finally got up the nerve to share my music with close friends and then performed some of my music at church. The response I received confirmed that the music was healing not only for me, but touched others as well. That's when recording a CD became my dream.

"It was never my dream to write music; but it was God's dream for me," Kristi says now in retrospect.

Finding the Dream from Despair

Kristi claimed Jeremiah 29:11 as her inspiration: "'I know the plans I have for you,' declares the LORD, 'plans to prosper you and not to harm you, plans to give you a hope and a future.'"

"When I decided to put my trust in God, He gave me hope through my music."

Kristi discovered her dream in the midst of deep despair. As she cried out to God, He handed her the dream as a way of coming back to Him.

"I was at the place in my life where I was on the brink of spiritual disaster," Kristi said. "Sometimes you can't see a path till you've reached the bottom. And that's where I was."

∽

That's often how it happens. When we are desperate for God, He shows Himself to us…and therein we find our purpose, our dream, and our ministry.

Dreams that develop out of our despair are frequently powerful dreams with the potential to reach many.

Today Kristi can relate to women who are struggling to find a sense of purpose, wrestling with depression, and crying out for something more. And in her music, she shares with them the answer: Jesus is our hope.

My friends Mitzi and Alex lost their baby daughter in a crib accident years ago. And today, this precious couple heads up a ministry in my church, training others to be lay counselors and care for those who are experiencing the deepest of hurts. Had they not endured that pain, they might not be the compassionate ministers to others that they are today.

Dreams that develop out of our despair are frequently powerful dreams with the potential to reach many. Perhaps that's why the enemy tried so hard to keep Kristi's from coming to fruition.

The Fight for the Dream

One morning, Kristi called me and spoke curtly.

"I've got some advice for your book on pursuing your dream," she said. "Don't pursue your dream; it will kill you. Go back to what's easy and never do *anything* with your life."

She was being sarcastic, of course.

She was in the beginning stages of recording her first CD. By this time she had written nearly 30 songs, and was selecting some for a CD. She sought a producer, lined up several musicians, and got ready to go. She experienced one open door after another on the journey to making her dream a reality. But just as it looked like her dream (to release to others the healing songs God had given her) was finally in sight, she hit the first stone wall of opposition.

During the first few recording sessions, Kristi got a taste of some hard realities associated with recording. "I felt like every personal weakness and imperfection I had was magnified in the recording process. Decisions had to be made regarding deadlines and changes to the music, and I needed desperately to find a balance between pursuing my original concept and taking advice from other skilled musicians. I failed miserably and gave in to almost every suggestion out of my own insecurity." Kristi felt that with each change that was made, the project unraveled more and more. Things started to fall apart and Kristi felt she was losing control of the situation. Suddenly, the project was no longer hers.

She came home frustrated one evening from a recording session, mad at herself for not standing for what she believed in.

"I was excited as plans were underway for recording. But I was also scared and intimidated and I wanted to make everyone happy. I started caring more about whether other people liked my music than whether I did."

Kristi admitted she had a problem with assertiveness. "Part of it was self-doubt. I was so willing to take advice from everyone that I started compromising the dream, and it turned into everyone else's project and not mine."

Kristi became frustrated by all the trouble she was encountering during the recording. "I was mad at God. I felt so inadequate. I didn't want to do it any longer," she said. "It wasn't my dream anymore."

Then the Dream Giver gently whispered to her heart: "Go back to the dream *I* gave you…that's the one you're supposed to pursue."

It was then that Kristi realized God was trying to nurture and strengthen her through the fight for her dream. He was allowing her to endure that testing, trying, and trusting phase (that we talked about in chapter 5) to see if she was really ready for what lay ahead. "I realized then that if all this was truly easy, it wouldn't be worth it."

Kristi took a deep breath and returned to a place of trust in her Dream Giver. She immediately halted production and reorganized the project and went back to the original songs as written. That Sunday, her decisions were confirmed. A person at church told her that one of the songs she sang in church months earlier was still resonating within her heart. Kristi realized it was one of the songs God had given her—a song that was being revised during recording. She then knew what God was trying to tell her. It was the original songs God gave her that she was to pursue, not the workings over of music that would be more marketable. It was God's dream for her that she was to pursue, not the dream others were trying to carve out for her.

With that confirmation, she went back into the studio with the basics of what she had started with and resumed recording. She could see now that when the songs were changed, the musicians hit a brick wall. But once she returned to her original work, the whole process smoothed itself out.

Whose Dream Is It?

If your dream is truly from God, then nothing on heaven or earth can keep you from reaching it. The Bible says, "If God is for us; who can be against us?" (Romans 8:31). Psalm 18:28-29 says that God keeps our lamp burning (thus keeping the passion alive), helps us advance against a troop (of those things that discourage us), and causes us to leap over a wall (the obstacles that loom before us to keep the dream from becoming a reality).

During the frustrations Kristi encountered while recording, she met her troop of doubts: "Everyone was frustrated. They were all looking at me. I was responsible; I was wasting everyone's time. I thought to myself, *What am I doing? I shouldn't be doing this. I'm out of my element.* All of a sudden, Satan was saying, "You shouldn't do this."

"Then I realized that God will allow us to be tested, and just because a circumstance might be hard, I don't have a right to quit. I know that if I don't give up, the test will make me stronger."

Kristi also realized that if she didn't pursue the recording of the songs, no matter how difficult it had become, she'd never be able to share her testimony through those songs. And that is the main reason she continues to pursue the dream. (Today, Kristi and I live out our dreams alongside each other as she joins me at "Longings of a Woman's Heart" conferences and retreats, performing some of her original songs.)[1]

Don't Give Up

Satan will do whatever he can to keep us from pursuing our dream. He'll subtly work on changing it until it's no longer the dream God gave us. Or he'll make the process of fulfilling our dream so difficult that we are tempted to give up. Or he'll discourage us so that we stop the pursuit and tell ourselves it's okay if we never go any further. But I believe the apostle Paul's words to the Philippians hold true for us when we're pursuing our dream: "For I am confident of this very thing, that He who began a good work in you will perfect it until the day of Christ Jesus."[2]

God won't leave us hanging halfway in pursuit of our dream. We might decide to give up; and if we do, it's because we gave up the dream ourselves, but God is not the one who gives up. If we let Him, He will give us whatever it is we need to keep going.

Keeping the Dream in Focus

Once you launch your dream, there will be times when the Dream Destroyer attempts to alter it, diminish it, or have you give up along the way. That's why it's so very important to clearly know that God is the One behind the dream. He will see you through to the end if you hang onto Him every step of the way.

Here are some steps that will help you keep your focus when the struggles start:

Remember Whose Dream It Is—If Kristi hadn't been convinced that the music was God's dream for her, she might've let the songs be twisted and shaped according to everyone else's desires. When you begin to get discouraged, go back to God in prayer and ask Him to reaffirm to you the original dream and how important it is to *Him* to see it through.

Recall Why You're Doing It—Whenever the dream becomes about us or our self-fulfillment, it becomes compromised because we can become easily satis-
fied with so much less than what God had intended for us. In my writing, I have to continually remind myself that the reason I write is for God's glory in meeting the needs of women with hurt-

I don't ever begin to believe that I was the one who got myself where I am.

ing hearts. When it becomes about me and my own self-fulfillment and advancement, then I will lose focus quickly.

Rely on God for Your Success—Pride is a big detractor on the way to our dream. It can creep into our lives and make us believe at any time that we're doing a great job of getting where we want to be. But as I've said constantly in this book, the dream is for the Dream Giver, not the dreamer. I've had to guard myself to make sure I don't ever begin to believe that I was the one who got myself where I am.

Right after my second book was published I was approached repeatedly by a prospective agent and other author friends who insisted that if I wanted to go further in my writing career, I needed to be represented by a person or agency.

I prayed about this and sought wisdom from my editor, and ultimately decided to go back to the original dream. The one thing that poured joy into my life was seeing how God handled the details of my writing and speaking ministry. I was in a place where I could credit no man, nor myself, for what He had given me. I realized then that to sign a contract that would make me dependent on another person or firm to further my career would be, for me, taking the ministry God had given me and giving it to someone else to manage.

While some authors have agents and still are able to keep a clear dependence on God, I knew that I wouldn't be able to. It would be too easy for me to look to someone else for my opportunities rather than to the Dream Giver Himself. To keep a healthy perspective, I determined that I would live by the motto that "God is my Agent." And He's been an excellent one thus far!

Staying on Course

You've come this far, my friend; don't back down now. Even when your circumstances become difficult, you have Someone going before you. If Kristi had given up on her dream when the going got tough, she would've given up on her purpose in life and her ability to stay where she needed to be with her Lord.

"If I'm not writing music, I'm not focused on God. And if I'm not on track spiritually, I can't write music," she said. "Writing music is such a big part of my link to God."

Living out our purpose often is. And with that in mind, we need to be all the more determined to stay on course with our dream—so that ultimately, God can be glorified because we're living according to how He designed us.

Dream On

1. Can you recall times of despair when God ministered to you in a particular way and convinced you of His plans for you?

   Could this be related to your dream, purpose, or ministry?

2. Can you relate to the struggle of having to fight for your dream? If so, how?

3. With your dream in mind, write out a couple thoughts that will help you:

   Remember whose dream it is:

   Recall why it is you're doing it:

   Rely on God for your success:

~ *Press On* ~

God tells us in Jeremiah 29:11 that He knows the plans He has for us, and He is not One whose mind and heart and plans for us will change. He wants to give us a future and a hope that involves living out our dream for His glory. When the winds of change and the struggles of life try to snatch away your desire to live out your dream, remember that the Lord tells us in 2 Corinthians 12:9, "My gracious favor is all you need. My power works best in your weakness" (NLT). If you're feeling weak, my friend, that's the point at which God's strength comes crashing through. At that point when you feel weakness coming on, remember these confidence-building words from Philippians 4:13: "I can do all things through Him who strengthens me" (NASB).

Part III

Protecting the Dream

"*[God] is able to do immeasurably more than all we ask or imagine....*"

—EPHESIANS 3:20-21

8
Avoiding the Dream Distracters

*I*f ever there was someone who could be distracted from their dream, it's my friend Marilyn. Marilyn is truly called to be a Bible teacher. Her passion for God's Word and her ability to teach it is clearly evident when she speaks. And Marilyn loves teaching God's Word.

But it seems the distractions work overtime when it comes to her living out her dream.

Marilyn struggles with poor health (she can be sick 25 out of any 30 days of the year), low self-esteem due to childhood abuse, and constant distractions that would have her doing *anything* but working toward the dream God has called her to pursue.

And yet, Marilyn is miserable when she's not being obedient to follow the dream God has placed on her heart.

"Obedience to the calling on my heart is the only way to find peace," she says. "I have to let go of how God is going to overcome all my obstacles and simply trust Him enough to obey what He tells me to do each day."

In the same way that the disciples responded to Jesus when He asked if they, too, would leave Him to go off and accomplish work of their own, Marilyn often says, "Where else is there to go, Lord?"

"Some days that is enough to keep me heading in the direction He is calling me."

It isn't that Marilyn doesn't want to follow the dream. She loves speaking to women's groups and teaching God's Word and would love to see her writing published someday as a means of getting her resources in the hands of others. But she is ever aware of the distractions that happen day in and day out to prevent her from working toward her dream. And a daily surrender to God's will in her life is the only way she can stay on track.

What Are *Your* Distractions?

You and I struggle with distractions on the way to our dream as well. You might be aware of them and you might not. We learned in chapter 2 how to dismiss the Dream Destroyer (Satan) and the different forms he takes to discourage us. But there are also a number of dream distracters lurking about us, which can be just as dangerous. These distractions might seem harmless at first, but if we aren't aware of them, and don't have a plan of attack against them, they can sideline us and affect our ability to give our all to living out our dream.

After interviewing several women about the chief distractions to living out their dream, I've come up with a list for you and me so we, too, can be on the alert against these enemies.

Busyness and Stress

Just about every woman I talk to struggles with busyness and stress. In my book *When Women Long for Rest* I address some of the reasons we feel so tired these days and how to get back to that place where we enjoy life and don't run the crazy harried pace of this world. The bottom line is that we can be as stressed and busy as we let ourselves become. Most of the time that stress rears its ugly head in my life when I've taken on too many commitments that are not within the realm of my dream and purpose.

At the end of chapter 1, you had the opportunity to put together a dream statement that could be referred to as your mission statement in life. When I first wrote out my dream statement several years ago, I was able to, for the first time in my life, focus my energies and time in that one single direction toward accomplishing my purpose. My statement was "To encourage, inspire, and motivate Christlikeness in women through writing, speaking, and teaching." Thus, when I was asked to lead a Bible study, I ran the request through that grid. Did leading a Bible study encourage, inspire, or motivate women to be more like Christ? And did it involve writing, speaking, or teaching? If so, I knew it was within the realm of my dream, and I would consider the task. But when I was asked to co-lead a community organization that had little to do with making my heart sing (like writing, speaking, and teaching God's Word), I passed on the opportunity.

You can prevent busyness and stress from interfering with your progress toward your dream if you know exactly what you want to do and stick to it. Also, plan into your schedule times of rest and recreation, as well as exercise, so you will be healthy enough to pursue your dream and less susceptible to being run down by overwork and stress.

Also, we need to make sure we don't become so busy doing things *for* God that we cease spending time *with* Him. How can we stay on the path of following our dream if we're too busy to hear the tender voice of our Dream Giver? I can easily lose my focus on the dream to write if I'm so busy that I begin to write in a mechanical manner simply for the sake of getting it done. Anyone can write, in a sense. But does God want me to be just anyone? And does He want me to write just anything? I've also learned it's quite easy to do certain things in "autopilot" and go through the motions without an engaged heart. And I don't *ever* want to resort to that.

Success

Success can be a big distraction when it comes to living out your dream. We live in a world that longs to make heroes of people. And in our flesh, we long to be indulged.

Author Os Guinness offers tremendous insight on this phenomena: "Today the media offer a shortcut to fame—instantly fabricated famousness with no need for the sweat, cost and dedication of true greatness. The result is not the hero but the celebrity, the person famously described as 'well known for being well-known.' A big name rather than a big person, the celebrity is someone for whom character is nothing, coverage is all."[1]

One of the traps we're vulnerable to when we follow our dream is that we can get so caught up with ourselves that we forget the One who got us where we are in the first place.

In Psalm 18:35 David said to God, "You stoop down to make me great." That verse tells me that we must not only humble ourselves, as we're instructed in James 4:10, but that we must also lift God up higher and higher so that He actually has to "stoop down" to get to us and lift us up.

When you and I are exalting God above everything else in our life, He delights in making us "great." And I suggest we keep the perspective that to be great in God's eyes alone is all that matters.

Criticism

It's strange how, even after we hear ten positive remarks in a day about the great job we've done, we will let one negative comment ruin our entire day. Why do we allow a single critical remark to affect us so greatly? We have to remember it's absolutely impossible to please all the people all the time. Learn from the criticism you hear, consider the source, then either consider it constructive or consider it no more.

Perceived Failure

The opposite of getting carried away with our success is the discouragement of perceived failure. There are highs, lows, and constants in everything...including the road we travel as we pursue our dream. If we are listening to the affirmation from heaven, we are less likely to be discouraged by our mistakes, failures, and perceived setbacks. In his book *The Dream Giver,* Bruce Wilkinson says, "Each stage or obstacle along our journey is intended not to *block* our dream, but to help us *break through* to the fulfillment God promises."[2] Remember that the mistakes you make can mold you into a wiser person and the setbacks you experience can ultimately make you stronger.

Procrastination

Probably the biggest culprit in all our lives is procrastination. If we have a lot going on, we tend to buy the line that we don't

> *A good plan today is better than a perfect plan tomorrow. If you're waiting for everything to be perfect, you'll wait most of your life.*

have time right now to follow through with our dream. Or, we'll work on it tomorrow. Pretty soon tomorrow turns into next week, then next month, then next year. There are dozens of reasons every day why we tell ourselves we can't get to work on our dream, and they usually end up being pretty lame reasons. It all comes down to prioritizing what's important so we don't put off that which really counts. Sometimes the perfectly clean house or the TV show we really wanted to watch has to wait.

Perfectionism

Have you ever told yourself that if you can't do it right, you're not going to do it at all? There's nothing wrong with having high standards for a project or goal. But I've heard it said that a good plan today is better than a perfect plan tomorrow. If you're waiting for everything to be perfect, you'll wait most of your life. And the perfect situation just might not come. So practice the motto "a good decision today is better than a perfect one tomorrow," and you'll find your bent toward perfectionism turning into straight-out productivity.

Lack of Patience

We want everything *now*. Sometimes the very thought of waiting for results turns us off altogether. If a project is going to require a lot of work or time, we tell ourselves, *I don't have that kind of time, I don't have the energy,* or *I don't think I can wait that long.* But anything worth something takes time. God waited 25 years to give Abraham a promised son. God waited 40 years to let the Israelites enter the Promised Land. God continues to wait, today, before allowing His Son to return to the world and make things right. One virtue that our pursuit of the dream teaches us is patience—a characteristic that God desires to cultivate in His people.

Feeling You're Too Old

I know we already covered this lie earlier, but the words, "I'm too old to do this" often surface in our minds even when we're well on our way to living out our dream. My friend Bonnie, whose journey toward her dream I described in chapter 2, remembers feeling in her forties that she was too old to begin pursuing her dream. "Now that I'm in my fifties, I wish I'd started pursuing it in my forties," she said in retrospect. Moses *started* leading the people of Israel when he was over 40. Caleb spied out the Promised Land, in full vigor, at 85 years old. Sarah was 90 before she finally became a mother. In light of God's track record of assigning special jobs to people who were well over 40, do you think that *God* thinks you're too old?

None of us are getting any younger. So move forward today, while you're younger than you're going to be tomorrow.

Lack of Money or Resources

I'm sure this distraction and source of discouragement hits every one of us at one time or another. Some dreams are expensive to pursue. To go back to school takes money and a certain amount of sacrifice. To start a business takes money. To invest in anything worthwhile seems to demand money. And if we wait until we have enough, we'll wait forever. Because none of us ever has enough! While we do need to be prudent and wise, and while it is never God's desire that we go into debt or spend money irresponsibly, most of the time the financial aspect of our dream comes down to a matter of faith.

Each time you get discouraged about where the money will come from, make your need a matter of prayer. The God who owns the cattle on a thousand hills (Psalm 50:10) is surely a God who can supply all your needs according to His riches (Philippians 4:19).

Pride/Ego

How does our ego distract us? When we don the "Superwoman" complex and believe we can do it all ourselves. Rather than look to others to help us along, we want to prove that we're capable and thus become "lone rangers." I can guarantee that if this is the case for you, you'll only wear yourself out and possibly fall short of your goal. There's always something someone else can do. Enlist people to pray for you as you journey toward your dream. Ask advice of others. Spend a day with someone who is living out your dream and learn from them how they got there. There are few "lone rangers" who reach their dream, and if they do, it's probably a self-centered dream. I'm convinced that dream work takes teamwork.

Assembling Your Dream Team

To get help in battling the distractions to fulfilling your dream, and to make sure you don't try to be a lone ranger, you need what

I call a Dream Team. Who do you have that can help you hold onto your dream when your arms start to get heavy?

In Exodus 17:8-15 we read that Moses sent Joshua and his men out to fight the Amalekites while he stood atop a hill, holding up his staff. As long as Moses' arms were raised, the Israelites were victorious in the battle. But when he became tired and had to drop his arms, the Amalekites started winning the battle. So Moses' brother, Aaron, and his friend, Hur, moved a stone beneath Moses for him to sit on and they each stood on either side of him and supported his arms so he could keep them in the air. Through that story, we learn that victory is often achieved with the help of others. It takes teamwork. We tire easily, and we need to have support on all sides of us—especially when the battle (or the distractions) gets intense.

So again I ask: Who do you have that can help you hold onto your dream? In chapter 2, I mentioned my sixth-grade school-teacher as my "Angel of Encouragement" who encouraged me to stay on track when my dream was about to be snatched from my heart. We all need angels of encouragement from time to time to not only help us hold onto the dream, but to keep us on track when we become distracted by the busyness and discouragement of everyday life.

Think for a moment about who is on your Dream Team. Maybe certain friends come to mind who are always cheering you on. Or maybe you haven't thought much about who is behind you, pushing you toward your dream. In that case, pray about whom God would have you approach about being on your "Dream Team." Then write out ways they can be a specific support to you at this time. Perhaps you need them to pray for your stamina when the journey looks difficult. Or maybe you need them to contact you once a week to make sure you've been disciplined about working through your dream to-do list. Whatever it is you need them to do, make sure they know. If they're good friends and they truly want your best, they'll be honored that you asked.

 ❧

Now that you're aware of some of the chief distractions that can hinder you from reaching your dream, you can focus on moving forward again. And as you do, remember the One who goes before you. There's a reason He's led you *this* far!

~ *Dream On* ~

1. Next to each of the major distractions listed, write a one-sentence plan for keeping your focus on the dream and overcoming the distraction:

    1. Busyness and Stress—

    2. Success—

    3. Criticism—

    4. Perceived Failure—

    5. Lack of Patience—

    6. Feeling too Old—

    7. Lack of Money—

    8. Pride/Ego—

2. Think of people who encourage you and inspire you to be all you can be. Who faithfully prays for you and cheers you in your victories and comforts you in your defeats? List them here…and either ask them to be a part of your team, or write them a note and thank them for the support they've been in your life.

My Dream Team:

3. Have you ever considered that your greatest encourager is the Dream Giver Himself? Write a prayer of thanks to Him now for all He has done in getting you to this point. And in that prayer, you may want to include a plea for help from the distractions that plague you the most. He, too, wants to see you focused on living out your dream for Him.

A Prayer to My Dream Giver:

Press On

How comforting to know that you are not alone on this journey! Scripture tells us that God goes before us into whatever circumstances or obstacles we may face. And our confidence, on those days when we're easily distracted, is found in Him, according to Isaiah 30:21: "Whether you turn to the right or to the left, your ears will hear a voice behind you, saying 'This is the way; walk in it.'" With that kind of gentle guidance, we don't have to lose sight of the dream that's before us.

"I used to ask God to help me. Then I asked if I might help Him. I ended up by asking Him to do His work through me."

—HUDSON TAYLOR

9
Encouraging Others to Live Their Dream

When I met Brenda—at a women's retreat, I noticed there was something special about her. She not only radiated with a love for God, but there was a depth to her. And I wanted to find out what it was. As I talked with her about the passion on her heart, I discovered she was a writer, too, and a Bible teacher. She loved God's Word and had a wonderful way of teaching and expressing it.

A woman after my heart, I thought.

That weekend wasn't a long enough time for me to get to know Brenda as well as I wanted to. But we had a chance to talk briefly about writing and speaking and her thoughts on writing a book. *If anyone should be writing and speaking, I thought, it should be her.* We kept in touch and I visited her home a few months later to give her some writing resources. She has since self-published her book *When Opportunity Knocks,* and her speaking and teaching ministry is now blossoming.

When Brenda crossed my path, she was ripe for encouragement. She wasn't seeking it out, as some do. I could tell, instantly, that she wasn't a "writer wannabe." She was instead a servant of God who was waiting on Him for the dream. The anticipation was in her eyes, but I had to pull out of her the verbal expression of the dream that God had placed on her heart.

If you look closely enough, you will spot those women, too—women who are ripe for encouragement in the area of pursuing their dream. No matter where you are in the process of discovering, pursuing, or living out your dream, there are always women around you who are one or more steps behind you in your journey. And those women need the same encouragement you needed when you were in their shoes.

My friend Pam saw in me an ability to write and speak and instantly became my cheerleader. On days when I felt no one else understood the setbacks, or on days when no one else shared in the extent of excitement I felt they should've, she was the one I called. And she always came through for me. I want to be that kind of encourager for other dreamers today. Not just to "do unto others as I would have them do unto me," but more as a gift to my Dream Giver. If I can help another one of His daughters see her potential for living out her dream, then I can give back to Him in a small way what He has so graciously given me.

Who Can *You* Encourage?

I told the story in chapter 2 about my sixth-grade schoolteacher who helped encourage me when I was ready to give up on my dream. And I believe God has given me opportunities since then to be an encouragement to others in the area of their dream. Can you think of women who come across your path who might need encouragement in discovering, pursuing, or living out their dream? We're sure to find women in all three stages. And when we do, it's time to offer to them the same life-giving hope that we found when God showed us His dream for us. Ask God to show you the women who are living on the edge of their dream, searching for more, or unaware of what God may be wanting to do with their lives. It could be *your* encouragement that causes them to take that step toward living out what their Creator designed them to do. Wouldn't that be a wonderful gift to your Dream Weaver…as a thank-you for how He's helped you as you pursue your dream?

When I reached out to Brenda and encouraged her, she encouraged me as well. Ours was a mutual ministry, and you can enjoy the same as you encourage other women. Brenda recently shared with me the Scripture verses that have encouraged her to stay the course and not give up. I probably never would have related those verses to the whole concept of pursuing one's dream:

> We are saved by trusting. And trusting means looking forward to getting something we don't yet have—for a man who already has something doesn't need to hope and trust that he will get it. But if we must keep trusting God for something that hasn't happened yet, it teaches us to wait patiently and confidently.
>
> ROMANS 8:24-25 (TLB)

Another translation of those encouraging verses reads:

> That is why waiting does not diminish us, any more than waiting diminishes a pregnant mother. We are

enlarged in the waiting. We, of course, don't see what is enlarging us. But the longer we wait, the larger we become, and the more joyful our expectancy" (MSG).

Just as fulfilling as discovering our dream and living it out is seeing others discover *their* dream and witnessing them living it out.

A Lesson in Joy

Lori was in my women's discipleship group last summer. And one day she was particularly down. She needed prayer about getting a job. She'd applied to several department stores, but was told she was overqualified. Before she'd quit her last job to give birth to her son, who was now just a year old, she was making two or three times the amount of money that was being offered for some of the jobs for which she applied. She wasn't expecting the same kind of pay again; she just needed to help make ends meet at home. She also needed a job with flexible hours so her teenage daughter could watch her infant son after her daughter was out of school.

"The employers I've contacted won't let me work for $6 an hour because they think I'm overqualified. So I sit at home making nothing per hour because of all my skills. That's nonsense," she exclaimed. "And, I need a job with flexible hours, yet very few jobs are able to flex with the hours I need to be at home with my family."

The other women and I appreciated Lori's sense of humility and willingness to work anywhere, but my friend Ginny beat me to the real question:

"Lori, what do you really *want* to do?"

That's when I chimed in. "Yeah, if you could have *any* job in the world, what would it be? What would just make your heart sing?"

Lori smiled, and her eyes brightened as she said, "I'd love to work in a nursery. I've always loved gardening. I could spend all day working with plants in my garden. To get paid to work with plants would be incredible."

"Then we're going to pray for a job that has you working with plants," I responded.

Lori was quick to give us all a dose of reality. "But all the nurseries want someone who has studied horticulture and has experience. I don't have any qualifications. I just love to work with plants."

We all took turns telling Lori how very much her heavenly Father cared about the desires of her heart. And perhaps He wanted to show her, through this request, that even something as small as "working with plants" was something He cared about if she cared about it.

So we all prayed, to the point of tears: "Lord, we know you love Lori and if she has to leave the house to work, you want her to be doing something she was *created* to do. God, would you show her, through this request, that You care about even the tiniest details of her life? And confirm to her that something as important to her as enjoying her job is something that's important to You, too."

Because Lori had struggled in the past with feeling loved and accepted by God, we all knew that how God answered this prayer request could have a *huge* impact in Lori's life and would demonstrate to her the kind of God He is. We all wanted to see her changed through how God would respond.

And, get this…God came through!

That very evening, I got an email from a friend at church. Because it was a "mass email," and it had been "forwarded" to me, I normally would not have opened it and taken the time to read it. But the subject line said "job offer" and I thought that perhaps it might be *something* Lori could apply for. As I read through the email, my mouth dropped open and tears came to my eyes: It was a posted job announcement from the community college in town asking for a horticulturalist's assistant. The ad read: "Do you love working with plants? Would you like to gain the experience needed to someday work in horticulture? Fun job. Meet new people. No experience necessary. Flexible hours."

I called Lori and excitedly told her about it.

All she could do was laugh and say, "Oh my gosh…"

The next morning, Lori called and inquired about the job. She would be caring for plants and gardens on the expansive estate homes of people in North San Diego County. She'd be doing what she loved to do, and she ended up working for a Christian woman who became a very good friend. In addition, the hours were extremely flexible and could accommodate the needs of Lori's husband and three children.

God has a way of renewing the joy in our lives every time we see someone else grasping hold of and living out their dream.

Not only did Lori get her dream job, but Lori and the rest of us in the discipleship group saw firsthand how our Creator so lovingly hands His children the desires of their heart when they seek Him in prayer, wide-eyed in anticipation of what He will do. (By the way, I thanked my friend at church for sending me the email that posted the job, and shared with her the wonderful story of how it was God's answer to Lori's prayer. My friend said she wasn't sure why she received that job post from the college in the first place, and when she passed it on to others, I wasn't on the list of intended recipients! She was surprised, to say the least, and couldn't imagine *how* I received that email.)

At the times when I start to doubt that God is so intimately acquainted with all our ways, I remember the story of Lori and God's love. And it reminds me, again, of His unfathomable ways!

I can honestly tell you that it was just as exciting to see Lori land that job as it was to hear from my editor the news that a proposal I had submitted had been accepted for publication and would become my very first book! God has a way of renewing the joy in our lives every time we see someone else grasping hold of and living out their dream.

Wouldn't you like to be a part of that, too?

Ways to Encourage Others

In Luke 7:36-50, we read of a sinful woman who anointed Jesus' feet with perfume and then cried at His feet, kissed them, and wiped them dry with her hair. The religious leaders who were dining with Jesus at the time were repulsed at the woman's actions. But Jesus made the point that because the woman was forgiven much, she loved much. She was extravagant in her expression of gratitude toward Jesus, and it touched His heart.

I can't help but think of that picture in terms of God handing us our dream. We did not deserve it, nor can we take credit for doing anything to obtain it. But the thought that a holy, sinless God would hand us imperfect people a dream He wants us to live out for His glory should cause us to weep at His feet, feeling unworthy yet grateful. And because we've been given so much, we should likewise want to give much back. One way to give back to Him is by helping others discover their dream and rejoicing with them when they recognize what that dream means to their life. Then we've led one more woman to the feet of Jesus to worship Him extravagantly because of what He's done for *her*, too.

Would you like to help others find that special place of worship at God's feet because of how He's revealed to them the dream on their heart?

Here are a few ways you can be that "angel of encouragement" to every woman you encounter:

Lift Up Others Through Your Words—This world is full of discouragement. I'm convinced the average woman hears more complaints than compliments in a day. If you set your mind to encourage each woman you encounter on a daily basis, God can use you to speak His words of encouragement to hearts that might not otherwise hear Him. Colossians 4:6 says to "let your conversation be always full of grace, seasoned with salt," and Ephesians 4:29 exhorts us to only say "what is helpful for building others up according to their needs, that it may benefit those who listen." Think about it. You can be an instrument of God simply by speaking kind words that build people up. I've heard incredible stories of the power of a positive word or two in some lonely people's lives. Ask God how you can encourage each person you see today. And you might be amazed at what ends up coming out of your mouth.

Look for Ways Women Excel—and then tell them. The enemy wants nothing more than to keep people in the dark about what

God wants them doing. And when you come along and tell someone she is shining brightly in a certain area, you will bring joy to her heart. Your encouragement may cause her to take a second look at what she is doing and what its purpose is in her life. I especially like to do this when I see young children or teenagers using their talents for the Lord. They are at a stage in their life when they're hungry for direction and most susceptible to suggestion. What if you helped plant a seed in them that blossomed into their dream years later? What a privilege and a blessing...and it takes so little effort.

Lend Your Resources—This may mean books, tapes, or just some helpful advice. You know how much it meant to you when someone was able to offer you suggestions or counsel that you needed at just the right time. If you don't have materials you can share, perhaps you can help the other person discover where to find the needed resources. For example, you could offer to go with that person to the library, or to some other place to help find the resources that person needs. Again, sometimes all it takes is a little encouragement to get someone going.

Investing in Others

As you begin to invest in others, you will see God take you another step further in your dream as well. When we focus on serving, we will be a conduit through which His gifts and blessings flow, rather than a dam that stops and clogs up whatever it is God wants to do through us.

When you begin passing on what you've learned and the blessings you've received, you're proving to your Creator that you understand the concept that it's all about Him and what He wants of you.

Dream On

1. Write a list of one to three women who could use encourage-
    ment right now in pursuing their dream.

2. Now, write a plan for what you will do this week to encourage
    them. (You may want to get them a copy of this book, and
    perhaps offer to go through a chapter a week with them,
    encouraging them to write out their answers in the application
    sections at the end of each section, as you have done. Imagine
    what an encouragement that could be to someone who is just
    a few steps behind you in discovering her dream.)

3. Write down two or three points that have encouraged you in
    this book so you will have them handy for encouraging
    others. You may also want to record the most helpful and
    encouraging Bible verses you've found in this book, or write
    some favorite verses of your own.

4. Pray now for the person(s) you listed, asking God to open a
    door for you to be a source of encouragement in her life and
    a helper in her pursuit of her God-given dream.

~ *Press On* ~

Do you realize that the very act of coming along-side another woman and helping her discover her dream could, in itself, be part of the dream God has given you? Remember, when we're obedient to the call, God often reveals to us another aspect of our dream, which we may initially think has nothing to do with our dream in the first place. Bless your heart, my friend, for being willing to help another woman discover what you've learned on your journey! As you care for the people on God's heart, He will continue to nurture yours.

"I'm thanking you, GOD, from a full heart,
I'm writing the book on your wonders.
I'm whistling, laughing, and jumping for joy;
I'm singing your song, High God."
—PSALM 9:1-2 (MSG)

10

Giving Glory to the Dream Giver

As a little girl, Lorelle dreamed of the day she would be famous.

"The dream that I have always wanted to pursue was to be on television," she said. "As a little girl I simply wanted to be famous. I *felt* famous. I feared no audience of any size or age, and I won public speaking trophies while in elementary school."

But over the years, God defined that dream in Lorelle's heart and made it about Himself, not her.

"As I got older, this dream matured and acquired a fueling passion: my faith—and sharing it with others. It wasn't all about me being famous anymore. It was *God* who I wanted to be famous." Like the prophet's proclamation in Isaiah 26:8, Lorelle's prayer became, "Your name and renown is the desire of my heart."

"My dream remained, but my motivation had changed. Now my dream was linked to a higher purpose, as I believe all God-given dreams are. I sincerely wanted to be in a place of influence for His name's sake."

Lorelle graduated from college with an education degree and worked as a substitute teacher for a couple of years. All the while, her prayer was, "Lord, maximize Your glory in my life. Position me where I will be most effective for You."

And He did.

Through a friend of hers who stepped out of a television job on maternity leave, Lorelle got an interview for a Christian television network. She ended up getting the job and within a couple months found herself hosting a program with other Christian women.

"God is so good—I have felt His peace and presence since the very first show we recorded. And in between recording shows, He is constantly reminding me to remain faithful in the little things, which serves as an anchor for me as I continue to mature along with the dream He has given me."

At 27 years old, Lorelle is one more woman who understands the concept that the dream belongs to the Dream Giver and her purpose is to glorify Him in all that she's been given.

God's Will Over Our Own

What did Lorelle and all the women, whose stories I've recounted in this book, have in common? They all wanted God's will over their own. That was what unlocked the door to their dream.

Psalm 37:4 says, "Delight yourself in the LORD and He will give you the desires of your heart." Proverbs 16:3 says, "Commit your works to the LORD and your plans will be established" (NASB). In Psalm 84:11 we read, "No good thing does he withhold from those whose walk is blameless." And in Matthew 6:33, Jesus said,

"Seek first his kingdom and his righteousness, and all these things will be given to you as well."

The principles are there: Delight in Him. Commit your plans to Him. Walk blamelessly before Him. Seek Him first.

I remember a time in my life when I wanted the dream...for me. I think we all do at one time or another. But a dream for just me is not big enough. It is empty. It is vain. It is meaningless. It dies when I do. And sometimes a lot earlier. A dream for Him lives on through the annals of time and echoes throughout the halls of eternity. That's the most exciting part of living out His dream for us. It becomes a legacy. And only things done for His glory truly live on.

A Way of Worship

When you and I are living out our dream, our lives can be summed up with one word: worship. For when we are truly living His dream for us, we are living out a form of worship.

When Bonnie (from chapter 2) is encouraging others and making them feel worthwhile in God's eyes, she is offering up worship to her Lord. When Kelly (from chapter 3) shines on the television screen, speaking of God's grace in her life, she is offering to Him a life

When God reveals to us the dream, there is no more appropriate response than worship.

of worship. When Peggy is sharing the gospel of Christ in Russia and when Lori is anchoring the news, both are offering to the Lord all they are in worship.

When Kristi sings, when Marilyn speaks, and when Brenda teaches God's Word, they are each offering up themselves in worship to their Maker by living out what He has called them to do. All the women whose stories I recounted in this book have wanted, more than anything else, to please the One who had whispered the dream on their heart. Before they knew there was a dream, they loved the Dream Weaver. Before they heard the call, they had connected with the Caller. Before they had plans and dreams of what they wanted, they wanted Him first.

When God reveals to us the dream, there is no more appropriate response than worship. And as we live out our dream, we continue to worship Him and bring glory to His name. God created us for His pleasure and He delights in our worship of Him. I believe it's safe to say that His dream for every one of us is that we know what it means to truly worship Him...in the way that He has called us to.

Women Who Left a Legacy

Look with me at what happened with the women of the Bible when they focused their whole hearts on worshiping the living God. Not only were their hearts calmed, but history was altered...and God's heart was pleased. And each of these women, in worshiping fully, seemed to be living out their dream.

Miriam, overwhelmed with joy and praise for her God, who had just parted the Red Sea so her people could walk through on dry land, felt an urge within her to break forth in praise. Something told her that if she missed this opportunity to worship the most high God, she'd regret it for the rest of her life. She picked up a tambourine and began to sing to her Deliverer. Her uninhibited praise was contagious. In the biblical account of her song in Exodus 15 we're told *all the women* followed her, picking up their tambourines, singing and dancing unto the Lord. Miriam's love for God and her desire to show it resulted in a moment of glory for the nation of Israel that her brother Moses years later penned into Scripture for all the world to read. As she lifted up her voice and caused the desert canyons to echo with the sounds of praise, a portion of biblical history was written.

∽⌒

Hannah, in awe that the Lord would open her barren womb and give her a child, offered to God the sacrifice of praise as she was giving back to God her young son, Samuel, so he could be raised in the temple as a prophet of the Lord. While she was giving up what was closest to her heart (her only baby boy), she sang from a heart not of resentment, but of love and trust. Hers is a song of beautiful imagery: "There is no rock like our God…He raises the poor from the dust and lifts the needy from the ash heap; he seats them with princes and has them inherit a throne of honor." Hannah's song was not only recorded in Scripture, but was centuries later echoed by Mary when she discovered she was carrying within her the blessed Messiah.[1]

∽⌒

Mary of Bethany must have known something that the others didn't. Perhaps that day she sat at Jesus' feet—while her sister Martha was busy bustling about the kitchen—she discerned Jesus' true mission here on earth. Because when Jesus came to her house again—and while Martha was bustling about yet again—Mary brought out some expensive perfume and poured it on Jesus' feet, wiping His feet dry with her hair. Mary's display of worship was so extravagant it caused one of the disciples to grumble that she had been wasteful. Yet Jesus said, "Leave her alone. She did it in preparation for my burial….I will not be here with you much longer."[2] Mary showed to Jesus a devotion so great that He commended her and said, "Wherever the good news is preached throughout the world, this woman's deed will be talked about in her memory."[3]

When was the last time you were so overwhelmed with love and praise for God that you responded as Miriam did? Can you recall a time that you wrote a song and sang it with all your heart to your Maker and Sustainer, much like Hannah? Is your worship of God so extravagant that it could be misunderstood by others, as was the case with Mary?

When you are living out your dream, that is what your life will look like: extravagant worship of the one true God.

What did Miriam, Hannah, and Mary have in common? Their gratefulness to God was expressed in extravagant worship. Would you say that you, too, know how to worship in such a way that it transforms you and leaves a mark on this world? If you are truly living out your purpose, you will know what it means to live for God in a way that makes your heart sing and to make all you do an offering of praise and worship to Him.

It's All for Him

In case you've gotten this far in the book and still are not sure what your specific calling or dream is, I want to encourage you to put yourself in the position where God can glorify Himself through you. When you do so, you will be in a place where you are living out His dream for you.

For most Christians, when it comes to discovering our part in the work of God's kingdom, the question we ask is self-centered: "What can I do for God?" The question we should be asking is God-centered: "What does God want to do through me?"[4]

With this in mind, I want to leave you with three steps you can take, anywhere and anytime, to become a woman who is living out God's purposes through you...whether it be through one specific dream He has placed on your heart, or through a number of ways He would like to be glorified in and through your life. You can start—and continue—to live out God's purpose for you by taking these three actions:

1. *Seek God's Will in Where He Would Have You*

Ultimately God wants you to be obedient. He desires that you be willing to say, "Send me, Lord. Not my will, but Yours." Remember Peggy in chapter 4? She had no intention of going to Russia, but every intention of being obedient to God's call on her heart. What she didn't expect was that where God would call her is where she would ultimately discover her dream. You seek His will, too, and wait for and see what He reveals to you.

Ask God: "What is my first step, Lord? You know my agenda. What's Yours? What are You going to lay on my heart that You want me to follow through on? Where do You want to lead me?"

2. *Step Out and Connect Somewhere*

We can sit around forever and wait for God to drop a dream into our laps. But God doesn't tend to work that way. God works in community. As Bible teacher Henry Blackaby says, "There's a corporate dimension to everything God does in your life. Every gift He has given is to be shared within the life of His people. If we aren't actively building up the [church], we aren't functioning as God desires."[5] So hook up with other believers in your church. Get into a small group Bible study. Begin to be where God's people are. Chances are you will not only cross paths with some who may be discerning as to your dream, but you will learn...and put yourself in the position where God can burden your heart with a cause or conviction that He wants you to begin to live for.

3. *Serve for a Season*

A sure way to discover your dream is to try many things...and see what happens. Again, God wants to see that we're willing to serve. The dinner I made for the missionaries wasn't as important to God as the fact that I was willing to do it. And thus, He opened a door for me to step into my dream. When you are faithful in a little, He will give you more. The true definition of a dream God whispers on your heart is one that He does through you...and we often don't discover that until we're in a position of serving Him and others.

Live It Out

As you seek God's will, step out and connect with others, and serve for a season, you will keep a heart bent on obedience. And an obedient heart is ready to live out one's dream.

So...it's time, my friend, to look at the world in front of you and embrace the wonderful opportunities that exist. God placed you here for a reason, and He desires that you live your life in such a way that you love Him and enjoy Him forever. What better way to do that than to approach life full of anticipation that the One who made you has a marvelous plan and He delights in watching you live it out? What pleasure His heart must feel as He watches what happens when you discover your dream!

Dream On

1. In what areas of your life do you need to seek God's will?

2. List a couple ways you can step out and connect within your church in your endeavor to discover how God wants to use you corporately.

3. Write a prayer here to God, telling Him that you want to be available to serve for a season in whatever area He may desire.

⁓ *Press On* ⁓

You can be the woman of God's dreams by living life to the fullest in an expression of worship. Paint for Him, dance for Him, nurse others back to health for Him, write for Him, teach for Him. Whatever He has given you to do, do it all for the glory of God.

Colossians 3:17 in The Message says, "Let every detail in your lives—words, actions, whatever—be done in the name of the Master, Jesus, thanking God the Father every step of the way." Shine brightly, oh dreamer, for this Dream Giver of yours. And *you* will be the woman of *His* dreams.

Notes

Once Upon a Dream

1. Ephesians 2:10 NLT.

Chapter 1—Daring to Dream Again

1. Os Guinness, *The Call* (Nashville, TN: Word Publishing, 1998), p. 31.
2. In John 10:10, Jesus said, "I have come that they may have life, and have it to the full."
3. Guinness, p. 14.

Chapter 4—Developing an Obedient Heart

1. Exodus 4:13.

Chapter 5—Being a "Big Dream" Believer

1. Jeremiah 1:4-10.

Chapter 7—Fighting for the Dream

1. Kristi's CD, *More than a Dream*, is available at her website: www.kristifoss.com. For information on our appearances together, go to her website or my site at www.cindispeaks.com, or see "An Invitation to Write" on page 163.
2. Philippians 1:6 NASB.

Chapter 8—Avoiding the Dream Distracters

1. Guinness, p. 83.
2. Bruce Wilkinson, *The Dream Giver* (Sisters, OR: Multnomah Publishers, 2003), p. 70.

Chapter 10—Giving Glory to the Dream Giver

1. Hannah's song is found in 1 Samuel 2:1-10.

2. John 12:7 NLT. (This is a different account than the one described in chapter 9 of the sinful woman anointing Jesus' feet with oil and crying at His feet and wiping them with her hair. The responses are similar, but the motivation in the two stories is different. The sinful woman was seeking repentance. And in this instance, Mary of Bethany was seeking to anoint Christ for His burial.)

3. Matthew 26:13 NLT.

4. Henry & Mel Blackaby, *What's So Spiritual About Your Gifts?* (Sisters, OR: Mulnomah Publishers, 2004), p. 11.

5. Blackaby, p. 21.

An Invitation to Write

What is the dream God has whispered on your heart? And how has this book helped you to discover or pursue that dream? Cindi would love to hear from you and know how she can pray for you and encourage you in this pursuit. You can contact her online at Cindispeaks@msn.com or write:

Cindi McMenamin
c/o Harvest House Publishers
990 Owen Loop North
Eugene, OR 97402-9173

If you would like Cindi to speak to your group, you can contact her and receive more information about her speaking ministry at www.cindispeaks.com.

When Women Walk Alone

Every woman—whether she's single or married—has walked through the desert of loneliness. Whether you feel alone from being single, facing challenging life situations, or from being the spiritual head of your household, discover practical steps to finding support, transforming loneliness into spiritual growth, and turning your alone times into life-changing encounters with God.

Letting God Meet Your Emotional Needs

Do you long to have your emotional needs met, yet find that your husband or those close to you cannot always help bring fulfillment to your life? Discover true intimacy with God in this book that shows how to draw closer to the lover of your soul and find that He can, indeed, meet your deepest emotional needs.

When God Pursues a Woman's Heart

Within the heart of every woman is the desire to be cherished and loved. Recapture the romance of a relationship with God as you discover the many ways God loves you and pursues your heart as your hero, provider, comforter, friend, valiant knight, loving Daddy, perfect prince, and more.

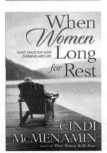

When Women Long For Rest

Women today are tired of feeling overwhelmed by all the demands on their lives and are longing for rest. They want to do more than just simplify or reorganize their lives. *When Women Long for Rest* is an invitation for women to find their quiet place at God's feet—a place where they can listen to Him, open their hearts to Him, and experience true rest.